Read and Think!

A Reading Strategies Course

2

PEARSON
Longman

Ken Beatty

Published by
Longman Asia ELT
2/F Cornwall House
Taikoo Place
979 King's Road
Quarry Bay
Hong Kong

fax: +852 2856 9578
email: pearsonlongman@pearsoned.com.hk
www.longman.com

and Associated Companies throughout the world.

© Pearson Education Asia Limited 2004

All rights reserved; no part of this publication may be reproduced, stored in a retrieval system, or transmitted in any form or by any means, electronic, mechanical, photocopying, recording or otherwise, without the prior written permission of the Publishers.

First published 2004
Reprinted 2006
Produced by Pearson Education Asia Limited, Hong Kong
GCC/04

ISBN-13: 978-962-01-8398-0
ISBN-10: 962-01-8398-3

Design Manager:	Winnie Sung
Editors:	Gregg Schroeder, Mark Horsley
Designer:	Waimann Lee
Illustrators:	Brian Wan, Waimann Lee

Thanks to Audio Producer David Pope and Sky Productions; voice artists Arvin Robles, Ben Pelletier, Melissa Nesbitt, Sheri Dorfman, Jovelyn Fuego and Ken Beatty.

The Publishers and author are grateful to Ed Regis, for his permission to reprint copyright material of quotations of Economist Julian L. Simon, originally published in "The Doomslayer," by Ed Regis, Wired website, Issue 5.02, The Conde Nast.

We are grateful to Corbis for permission to reproduce copyright photographs.

Author acknowledgments
A great many people worked hard to make this book a success, including all those who gave suggestions on early drafts and outlines. Great thanks go to my meticulous and creative editor Gregg Schroeder for thoughtful drudgery during weekends and late nights, to Mark Horsley for editorial support and to Waimann Lee, who organized words into visual ideas.

Thanks also to my colleague at City University of Hong Kong, Nicola Gram, for her help.

As always, I thank my wife Ann for unceasing support and beg forgiveness of my sons, Nathan and Spencer, for lost play.

The publisher's policy is to use **paper manufactured from sustainable forests**

Introduction to students

Getting the most out of *Read and Think!*

Do you like to read? Would you like to read better?

Reading is more than just knowing a lot of words. When you read different kinds of texts, you need to know what strategies and skills to use. You also need to have a basic knowledge of different disciplines, such as university subjects.

Read and Think! is a four-level series to help you improve your reading. It's made up of many different parts. Each unit is divided into two lessons. Each lesson features an interesting reading passage. The passages included are presented as articles, movie reviews, letters, plays, poems, speeches and stories.

The two passages in each unit give two points of view on the same topic. The topics are followed by different kinds of exercises, such as fill-in-the-blanks, multiple choice, matching and short answer. Once you've finished the unit, you have a chance to show what you know by discussing debate topics.

Reading is not just a skill for words, but also for images. So, to make the book more interesting for you, cartoons, charts, diagrams, illustrations, maps and photos are included, with activities to help you think.

Throughout each unit, help in the form of *Reading strategies, Language notes, Exam strategies, Debate strategies, Computer notes* and *Culture notes* is provided. Special *Concepts* boxes expand on core ideas within readings and *What about you?* sections let you think about how the topic of the unit relates to you.

Beyond the book, topics for further study and online resources are included on the companion website. Your teacher can also help you measure what you learn by using photocopied quizzes.

Reading is a lifetime skill—learn to do it well!

Ken Beatty

Introduction to teachers

Working with *Read and Think!*

Read and Think! is written by a teacher for teachers. The purpose of the four-level series is to help your students see reading as an interesting problem-solving activity. The series improves students' reading skills while covering issues important to students, including ethical and academic issues. These issues are presented in a variety of text types with carefully integrated graphics.

The four Student Books each offer twelve units. Each unit is divided into two lessons.

Level 1: 250–300 words per reading
Level 2: 300–400 words per reading
Level 3: 600–700 words per reading
Level 4: 800+ words per reading

Unit content
Each unit begins with a title and key words taken from general areas of knowledge, usually university disciplines.

Lesson One
- **Before you read** starts off with questions to make students think about the new topic. Ask students to discuss the questions in pairs or small groups or use them as a whole-class activity. A picture, map, diagram or illustration follows with something for the students to do. Use this to create more interest in the topic and explore new vocabulary.
- **Read about it** takes students into the first of the unit's two main readings. After listening, students read on their own. Finally, students read and listen together to match pronunciation with comprehension. Key vocabulary notes from the *Longman Active Study Dictionary* help students learn key words, and space at the back of the book is provided for students to write their own dictionary, adding unfamiliar words as they encounter them.
- **After you read** gives students a chance to show what they know by asking questions about the reading. An *Understand what you read* section on understanding what they read helps to explain a key point of learning English. The *What about you?* section helps students see their own place in the topic.

Lesson Two
- **Read about it** offers another perspective on the unit topic to help students think about what they read. Sometimes these second readings take the opposite point of view. Start off by listening to get the students involved. Ask students to listen with their books closed.
- **After you read** has a higher level task, such as summarizing a paragraph in one sentence, as well as fun activities, including word puzzles. This is followed by multiple choice comprehension questions.
- **Debate** gives students a chance to show what they know based on arguing a point made in the unit. Two perspectives on the same idea are given with supporting points and room for students to add their own ideas.

Strategies and *notes* help students with reading, language, culture and exams, and are found throughout the unit.

Other ***Read and Think!*** components include:
- Teacher's Manual, with teaching notes and answer keys
- CD of all passages
- CD-ROM Test Bank, which can be used to produce photocopy masters
- Website at **www.read-and-think.com**, with teacher and student support

Contents

Units	Lessons	Text types	Fields of study	Reading focus	Debate topic
1. The Search for Atlantis Page 1	1. Where Is the Lost City? 2. Evidence for Atlantis?	Articles	Geography Philosophy Mythology	Dictionary skills	Atlantis will eventually be found one day.
2. The Olympic Games Page 13	1. The Birth of the Modern Olympics 2. Olympic Tribulations	Articles	Tourism Leisure Sports	Thesaurus skills	The Olympics is a true sign of our civilization.
3. Reach for the Stars Page 25	1. A New Home in the Stars 2. Why Explore the Universe?	Letters	Astronomy Economics	Reading letters	Everyone should support space exploration.
4. The Lord of the Rings Page 37	1. Metaphors in *The Lord of the Rings* 2. The Creator of Middle Earth	Literary criticism Biography	Literature Biography Fantasy	Looking at metaphors	A few people who believe in the right things can change the world.
5. Small Is Beautiful Page 48	1. Buddist Economics 2. Anti-Globalization: Problems and Solutions	Articles	Environment Economics Sociology	Commas and periods	Globalization has helped make the world a better place.
6. Is Money Everything? Page 61	1. Healthy, Wealthy and Wise 2. Money Isn't Everything	Articles	Philosophy Psychology Business	Survey	Making money is the best way of achieving dreams.

Units	Lessons	Text types	Fields of study	Reading focus	Debate topic
7. What Killed the Dinosaurs? Page 73	1. Where Did They Go? 2. An Explosive End?	Theory Rebuttal	Paleontology Geology	Adjectives and adverbs	The same thing that killed the dinosaurs could kill us.
8. Looking for Lost Treasure! Page 84	1. Lucky Accidents 2. The Mystery of Oak Island	Articles	Cartography Archaeology History	Phrasal verbs	There are lots of treasures out there for people to find.
9. Into Battle! Page 96	1. The Battle of Agincourt 2. Band of Brothers	Article Speech	Military studies History	Conjunctions	There are always many sides to history.
10. The Future of Education Page 108	1. An Ancient and Modern University 2. The Growth of Asian Universities	Articles	Education Computing	Contractions	Universities continue to adapt to the needs of society.
11. Extinct! Page 120	1. Island Biogeography 2. How Many Species Become Extinct Each Year?	Articles	Biology Geography	Prepositions	People are destroying the world's environment.
12. Angels or Outcasts? Page 131	1. I Love Your Wings! 2. Making Outcasts	Articles	Psychology Sociology Medicine	Colons, em-dashes and semicolons	People should be able to change the way they look.

Appendix Page 142

The Search for Atlantis

Lesson One

UNIT 1
Geography
Philosophy
Mythology

Before you read

- What did this structure look like when it was new?
- What was it used for?

Why do you think this building was allowed to fall apart?

Ruins in Greece

Read about it

- Why is the city "lost"?
- What words sound like capitals, names, places and the first words of sentences?

Where Is the Lost City?

For more than a thousand years, people have wondered about the location of the lost city of Atlantis, a rich paradise once ruled by a wise king.

Plato is the person most closely thought of when talking about Atlantis. Plato (427–347 BC) was a student of the Greek philosopher Socrates (469–399 BC). Socrates was a very influential thinker, but when his ideas became too controversial, he was forced to kill himself by drinking poison. After he died, Plato traveled for a few years before returning to establish a school in Athens called the Academy. It has become the role model for today's universities. At the Academy, Plato taught the students through the use of debates, where two or more people took different sides of an argument. Often these debates used Socrates' stories as a starting point. Atlantis was a good example.

Socrates did not like writing. He thought that reading and writing made

Ruins of the Acropolis, Athens

Language note

BC (Before Christ) or BCE (Before Common Era) are used for dates before the year 1. The year 1 and later dates use AD (Anno Domini, meaning Year of our Lord) or CE (Common Era).

The Search for Atlantis

people stupid! Fortunately, Plato did not feel the same way, and his students copied down what Plato remembered of the teachings of Socrates. He described Atlantis as a culturally- and scientifically-advanced civilization that had existed long ago. The people of Atlantis had used their knowledge to enslave much of the world. Atlantis was finally defeated by Athens, but then all records of it were lost when a great flood destroyed both Athens and Atlantis.

Plato and Aristotle

Did Atlantis ever exist? Or was it just a story to show what happens to people when they become too powerful? If it did exist, where was it? One clue is that it was supposedly beyond the Pillars of Hercules, now known as the Strait of Gibraltar, somewhere in the Atlantic Ocean. Countless explorers, who have had their own ideas, looked everywhere from England to China. Perhaps you will find it one day or solve one of the other great unknown mysteries of the world. Perhaps you will find something that no one was even looking for.

(326 words)

Legend

a. Atlantic Ocean
b. Spain
c. Strait of Gibraltar
d. Mediterranean Sea
e. Egypt
f. Greece
g. Athens
h. Thera
i. The Black Sea
j. Italy

Reading strategy

Improve your reading comprehension by discussing what you read with a friend. Explain what you have read and add your opinions about the passage. Putting your ideas into spoken words helps you remember.

Reading strategy

To help with your reading comprehension, keep a personal dictionary where you list new words and phrases. Constantly review your new words.

Vocabulary notes

1. **civilization** (noun) a society that is well organized and developed
2. **culturally** (adverb) in a way that is related to a particular society and its way of life
3. **debate** (noun) an organized discussion on an important subject
4. **enslave** (verb) to make someone a slave
5. **philosopher** (noun) someone who studies and develops ideas about the nature and meaning of existence, truth, good and evil, etc.
6. **poison** (noun) a substance that can kill or harm you if you eat it, drink it, etc.
7. **supposedly** (adverb) used to say that you do not believe what you are saying about the thing or person you are describing, even though other people think it is true

Add new words to your personal dictionary on page 146.

Read and listen again to practice your pronunciation.

After you read

Computer note

Don't rely on your computer to take care of your spelling problems. Word processors don't recognize some words and ignore wrong words you may have typed, for example: *there*, *their* and *they're*. Check your work carefully.

A. Answer these questions.

1. What did Plato establish?
2. What was once the name for the Strait of Gibraltar?
3. How was Atlantis able to enslave other countries?
4. What two things destroyed Atlantis?
5. Why do you think people want to find Atlantis?

The Search for Atlantis

Understand what you read

Dictionary skills

English has too many words to keep them all in one dictionary. In fact, the English language is constantly growing, adding new words every day. Many words we use about computers, for example, did not exist 20 years ago. You may have many kinds of dictionaries: bilingual, thick and comprehensive monolingual, computer-based, pocket-sized. Choosing the best dictionary may depend on where you use it. If you need to take it to class, choose a smaller one that is easier to carry. If you mostly use it at home, get a larger one.

Here are four tips for working with your dictionary:
- When you read, try to understand by context, but keep a list of new words.
- Every time you look up a word, put a dot next to the word in pen.
- If you look up a word more than once, try to understand why it's a problem for you to spell or remember.
- Use the pronunciation guide to learn how to say a word correctly.

B. Circle the wrong words.

Around the world, there (our) many stories about great floods. Often, the floods are a punishment (bye) a god. A hero usually escapes to tell the storey and continue the human race. Is there any truth (too) the stories? Recent discoveries around the Black See show it suffered a terrible flood from the Mediterranean Sea around 5500 BC.

C. **Fill in the missing words. Use the correct form of the word.**

- **discern** (verb) to see, notice, or understand something
- **illustrate** (verb) to explain or make something clear by giving examples
- **model** (noun) someone or something that people want to copy because they are successful or have good qualities
- **mythical** (adjective) not real or true, but only imagined
- **satisfaction** (noun) a feeling of happiness or pleasure because you have achieved something or got what you wanted
- **social** (adjective) relating to human society and its organization, or the quality of people's lives

What do people hope to _discern_ from a lost civilization like Atlantis? Besides the _model_ of knowing a lost treasure actually exists, people may want a _illustrate_ for their own _social_ development. This may actually have been the point of Atlantis, a _mythical_ city of science and culture that was only meant to _satisfaction_ how people should live.

Why else might someone want to find the lost city of Atlantis?

What about you?

If you found directions to take you to Atlantis, could you follow them? Try following these directions and circle Atlantis: The biggest island, Macro, isn't Atlantis. The smallest island, Micro, isn't either. Micro is to the left of Medial. Between Medial and Distal is another island. Distal is next to the largest island. And Distal is between it and Atlantis.

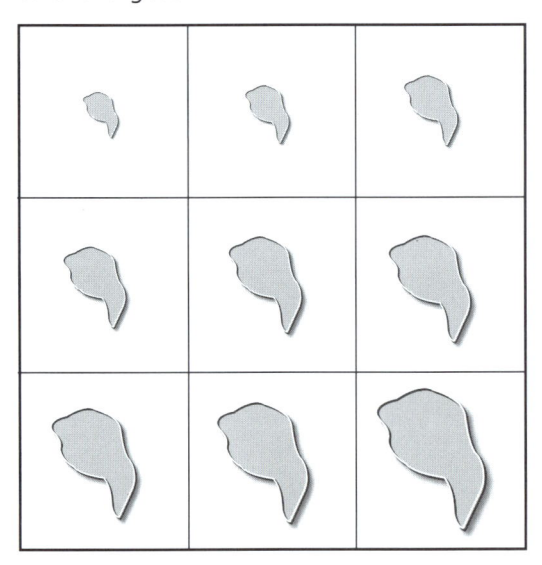

Lesson Two

Read about it

- What are different ways of discussing dates?
- Does the author believe or not believe in Atlantis?

Language note

Dates are grouped in *decades* (ten years), *centuries* (one hundred years) and *millennia* (one thousand years).

Evidence for Atlantis?

Modern technology has thrown out many claims related to the location of Atlantis. But it has also helped locate other important civilizations in Central American jungles. Using satellites, we can map the Earth's surface and help in excavations of what were once thought to be mythical civilizations.

In looking for evidence of Atlantis, people have tried to imagine what sort of remains such a civilization might have left. Certainly there would have been tools, probably made of metal.

It took a long time before the first people started to work with metal. First came the Stone Age, when most tools, such as axes and spearheads, were made of stone. The Stone Age lasted until about 3000 BC when people finally learned to create bronze tools and weapons, which were both stronger and lighter. This era, called the Bronze Age, lasted until the Iron Age began, around 1100 BC. Could this have been the age when Atlantis existed?

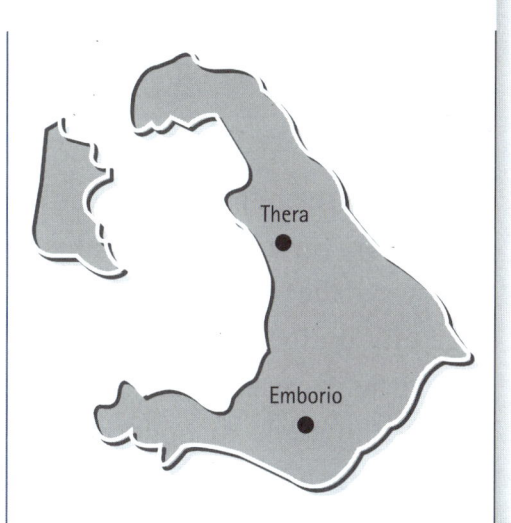

Reading strategy

Different writing types require different ways of thinking and so are written differently. You need to read a science text in a different way from a poem or a newspaper editorial. In the first example, you look for facts, in the second, you read for pleasure, and in the third, you examine opinions.

The island of Thera

In the late 1960s, a Greek professor, Spyridon Marinatos, discovered the remains of a Bronze Age city on the island of Thera. During his excavations of the city's streets, he made discoveries of buildings that were highly-developed structures. Within the homes and businesses were ceramics used for eating and storing food, and also colorful wall paintings. Together, all these discoveries indicate that the city was once a wealthy and culturally-rich society. Who knows how they might have developed had they continued until today? But, around the year 1500 BC, a great disaster struck: a devastating volcanic eruption ripped the island apart, probably killing everyone who lived there. Those who were not killed right away were buried along with the entire city under five meters of ash. The volcano also sent tidal waves around the Mediterranean, destroying other cities. The people of Thera disappeared from the face of the Earth.

Was Thera the land of Atlantis? Some believe that Plato was actually relating the story of Thera, but was mistaken about its location and the date of its destruction.

(335 words)

Excavating on Thera

The Search for Atlantis

Vocabulary notes

1. **bronze** (adjective) a hard metal that is a mixture of copper and tin
2. **ceramics** (noun) artistic objects made from clay
3. **devastating** (adjective) causing a lot of damage
4. **excavate** (verb) to dig up the ground, especially in order to find things from the past
5. **iron** (noun) a common heavy metal that is an element and used in making steel
6. **relate to** (verb) to be connected or concerned with something
7. **structure** (noun) something that has been built
8. **tidal wave** (noun) a large ocean wave that flows over the land and destroys things

Read and listen again to practice your pronunciation.

After you read

A. Summarize the main idea in one sentence.

What evidence would confirm the existence of Atlantis? Perhaps new written records and maps will be found someday or a chance discovery will be made by a submarine searching the oceans. Even then, unless the name "Atlantis" was written clearly somewhere on the city walls, some people will keep looking forever.

B. Vocabulary check: Fill in the missing letters to find the secret word.

					c	e	r	a	m	i	c	s		
	c	u	l	t	u	r	a	l	l	y				
					s	t	r	u	c	t	u	r	e	
		p	h	i	l	o	s	o	p	h	e	r		
						s	o	c	i	a	l			
					d	i	s	c	e	r	n			
				e	x	c	a	v	a	t	e			
					m	o	d	e	l					

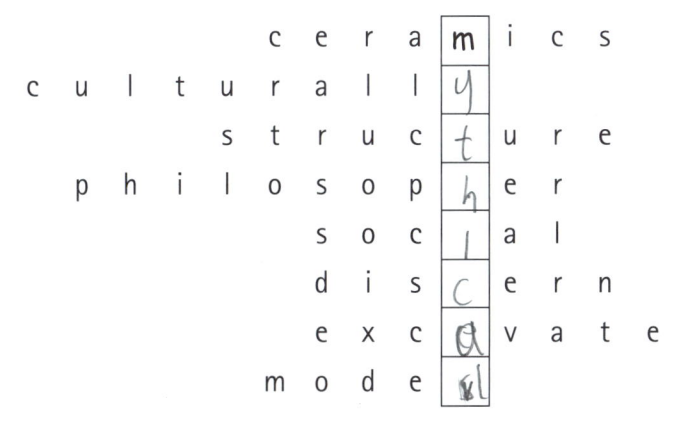

Language note

When you learn a new word, learn the other forms of the word at the same time. For example, *form*, *forms*, *formal*, *formative*, *formation*.

Culture note

Throughout history, there have been many imaginary places and monsters that people once believed in but were later explained or proven false. Why do people like to believe in things that aren't real?

9

C. **Choose the best answer.**

1. Atlantis was _c_.
   a. a university
   b. a person
   c. a city
   d. two small countries

2. Plato and Socrates were _a_.
   a. Therian kings
   b. Chinese explorers
   c. British slaves
   d. Greek philosophers

3. In the late 1960s _b_.
   a. Socrates killed himself by drinking poison
   b. Marinatos discovered the remains of a city
   c. Plato established the Academy in Athens
   d. explorers from England and China discovered the Strait of Gibraltar

4. The Stone Age, Bronze Age and Iron Age refer to _a_.
   a. the material people used to create tools and weapons
   b. the cities people lived in around the world
   c. the disasters that took place—volcanoes, tidal waves and floods
   d. the teaching methods of philosophers used in the universities

5. The age before people learned to work with metals was called _d_.
   a. the Iron Age
   b. the Bronze Age
   c. the Stone Age
   d. a, b and c

6. A question that is representative of the second passage might be _c_.
   a. Did Marinatos discover the Iron Age?
   b. Was Plato lying about Thera?
   c. Was the Iron Age a culturally-rich society?
   d. Is Thera the lost city of Atlantis?

7. All records of Atlantis were destroyed by a great _c_.
   a. earthquake
   b. flood
   c. volcanic eruption
   d. excavation

8. The passages suggest that Atlantis may be _a_.
   a. a mythical city
   b. an excavated city
   c. an enslaved city
   d. a devastated city

Exam strategy

When you read a multiple choice question, think of the answer before you look at the choices. Then choose the answer closest to what you thought.

The Search for Atlantis

Debate

Take one side, add your own ideas and debate in pairs or groups.

For: Atlantis will eventually be found one day, as long as we keep looking.
Points:
- Atlantis was once an ideal civilization and finding out about it will help improve our current civilization.

- Too many people have talked about Atlantis for it not to exist.

- Science will help us uncover Atlantis and its secrets.

- _____

- _____

- _____

Against: Atlantis was a myth that we should not waste time on any more.
Points:
- People like to believe in things that don't exist, such as the Yeti, Loch Ness Monster and vampires.

- Time spent looking for Atlantis could better be spent looking for more information about civilizations that did exist.

- Atlantis was only a story to be argued about, not a real place.

- Atlantis was only a myth no point to wasting time

- We spent too many time on Atlantis

- No result showing that Atlantis actully exift

Debate strategy

When you debate, make it very clear to yourself, your debate opponent(s) and everyone else who is listening, exactly what the debate is about—the *thesis*.

Say:
- "Today, I am (or *we are*) going to explain why … ."

Or begin with an introduction, explaining why it is important to debate the topic.
- "Many of you will have read in newspapers the shocking story of … ."
- "Today I am (or *we are*) going to explain what should be done … ."

Repeat your thesis at the end of your argument, summarizing your points.

Another idea to debate

It's easy to prove something exists, but how can you prove something doesn't exist? This is one of the problems of looking for Atlantis. In Asia, people have long believed in dragons but not found them. However, when we look for one thing, we sometimes find something else quite amazing. What were once thought to be ancient dragon bones have turned out to be the fossils of dinosaurs.

Learn more

Besides Atlantis, what are some of the other great mysteries of the world? Find examples and report them to your class.

Look online

Check out the website at www.read-and-think.com for extra learning resources.

Add new words to your personal dictionary on page 146.

The Olympic Games

Lesson One

UNIT 2
Tourism
Leisure
Sports

Before you read

- Who started the modern Olympic Games?
- When were the ancient Olympic Games first held?

What's happening in this photo?

The XXIII Olympiad, Los Angeles 1984

Language note

The Olympics are numbered with Roman numerals:
I = 1   II = 2
III = 3   IV = 4
V = 5   VI = 6
VII = 7   VIII = 8
IX = 9   X = 10
XX = 20
What is XXIX?

Read about it

- What sports are mentioned?
- Who was Pierre de Coubertin?

The Birth of the Modern Olympics

What are now called the ancient Olympic Games started in 776 BC, near Athens, Greece. These early games were based on even earlier games that were often held for important Greek festivals and weddings. The Greeks also liked to have games at funerals. These early games usually included races on foot and by chariot, as well as discus, boxing and wrestling. Many Olympic events were based on soldiers' skills.

The games were held every four years. During the games, athletes would come from all over Greece as well as from Greek colonies around the Mediterranean Sea. Many of the different Greek groups fought each other, but they would always agree to stop fighting so everyone could compete. After the games, they would continue their fighting.

The games continued to be held for more than a thousand years until 393

Greeks lighting Olympic flame, 1952

Reading strategy

An important reading strategy is summarizing; think about what you have read in shorter terms. Often summarizing is done by ignoring the examples and simplifying the main points.

The Olympic Games

Shot put, Antwerp 1920

Rowing, Los Angeles 1932

Swimming, Munich 1972

Weightlifting, Sydney 2000

Pierre de Coubertin

AD. At this time, Greece was ruled by the Romans, and the Christian Roman Emperor Theodosius decided to stop them. He did not like the Olympic Games because they honored Greek gods, not the Christian one.

The Greeks and many others tried for hundreds of years to start the Olympic Games again. But no one was able to do so. Finally, a young Frenchman, Pierre de Coubertin (1863–1937) succeeded.

De Coubertin was a great athlete. He liked to box, fence and ride horses. He rowed boats until he was seventy-two years old. As his father was an artist and his mother a musician, he kept art and music as part of the Olympics. In 1896, the first international Olympic Games were held in Athens. Athletes came from fourteen countries.

These first few Olympics were quite disorganized. Sometimes they lasted for months! They featured some of the ancient events, but also new events were introduced, such as golf, tennis and sailing.

(299 words)

Culture note

The Latin Olympic motto is *Citius, Altius, Fortius* meaning *Faster, Higher, Braver*. However, the usual English translation is *Swifter, Higher, Stronger*.

Vocabulary notes

1. **boxing** (noun) a game in which two men fight by hitting each other wearing big leather gloves
2. **chariot** (noun) a vehicle with two wheels pulled by a horse, used in ancient times in battles and races
3. **discus** (noun) a sport in which you throw a heavy plate-shaped object as far as you can, or the object that you throw
4. **disorganized** (adjective) not arranged or planned very well
5. **fence** (verb) to fight with a sword as a sport
6. **funeral** (noun) a ceremony for someone who has just died
7. **honor** (verb) to treat someone with special respect, because you admire them
8. **sailing** (noun) the activity of sailing in boats
9. **wrestling** (noun) a sport in which you try to throw your opponent onto the ground and hold them there

Add new words to your personal dictionary on page 146.

Listen

Read and listen again to practice your pronunciation.

Discussion

After you read

A. Answer these questions.

1. What sports do the ancient and modern Olympic Games have in common?
2. What led to the end of the ancient Olympics?
3. What does the phrase *he kept* suggest about the first Olympics?
4. Why might Athens have been the choice for the first modern Olympics?
5. Why might de Coubertin have wanted to restart the Olympic Games?

Understand what you read

Thesaurus skills

A thesaurus is a kind of dictionary that gives the same meanings (synonyms) and the opposite meanings (antonyms) of thousands of words. You most often use a thesaurus when you write, for example, when you have used a word such as *nice* several times in a paragraph and want to vary it. But a thesaurus can also be useful when you are reading.

Here are four tips for working with a thesaurus:
- Understand new words by looking at their synonyms and antonyms. They are sometimes more helpful than a dictionary definition.
- Be careful of different connotations—positive or negative messages. The words *slender* and *skinny* both mean the same thing, but *slender* is positive and *skinny* is negative.
- Never use a word from a thesaurus if you don't know what it means!
- Remember that longer words aren't always better words.

B. Find synonyms and antonyms in a thesaurus.

word	synonym	antonym
play (verb)	joinin	quit
compete (verb)	finish	fail
enjoy (verb)	happy	bad
race (noun)	game	
lose (verb)	defeted	win

Computer note

Your computer probably has a thesaurus. It's useful to use the thesaurus for checking the meanings of new words by finding their synonyms and, sometimes, their antonyms.

C. Fill in the missing words. Use the correct form of the word.

- **ancient** (adjective) happening or existing many hundreds of years ago
- **compete** (verb) to try to win something or to be more successful than someone else
- **high heels** (noun) women's shoes with a high heel
- **medal** (noun) a round, flat piece of metal given as a prize to someone who has won a competition or who has done something brave
- **sentence** (verb) to give a legal punishment to someone who is guilty of a crime
- **suit** (verb) to have the right qualities to do something

Girls and young women could watch the _ancient_ Olympic Games, but married women could not and could be _sentence_ to death if they were caught. Similarly, in the first modern Olympic Games in 1896, women could not compete. In the 1900 Paris Olympics, nineteen women _compet_ in three sports: tennis, sailing and golf. The first Gold _medel_ in Women's Golfing was won by Margaret Abbot who took the prize because all the French women golfers arrived in _high heel_ and tight skirts that weren't _suit_ to the game.

What part do women now play in the Olympics?

What about you?

Could you be an Olympic athlete? Perhaps. But an athlete has to spend a lot of time training. Look at some Olympic records on the WWW and see how you compare. For example, see how fast you run or swim 100 meters and compare it to the fastest Olympic time. How close are you to the strongest person in the world? See how much you can lift without hurting yourself.

Lesson Two

Read about it

- What are some negative points about the Olympics?
- What negative words are used to describe unfair practices?

Olympic Tribulations

The Olympic Creed says: *The most important thing in the Olympic Games is not to win but to take part, just as the most important thing in life is not the triumph but the struggle. The essential thing is not to have conquered but to have fought well.*

However, the Olympics have long been rocked by scandals involving almost everyone: spectators, judges, coaches and athletes. In several cases, judges have unfairly supported favored athletes instead of the true winners.

Some athletes have used tricks to cheat, such as at the 1976 Montreal Olympics. During these games, the world famous Soviet fencer Boris Onischenko was fighting against an American opponent. During fencing matches, a simple electric system in the fencing foils, or swords, is used to score points. A point was scored, but the American claimed that he did not feel he had

Soviet Boris Onischenko caught cheating, 1976 Olympics in Montreal

Reading strategy

To read more quickly, read once, skipping over all the words you don't know. Once you have a general idea of what the passage is about, go back and look up the words you don't understand.

been touched. The judges asked to look at Onischenko's foil. Inside was a tool that scored points without having to touch the opponent. The Soviet fencer quickly left and the American became the winner.

But the greatest problem has been prohibited drugs, used to make athletes stronger and faster. Drug abuse in the modern Olympics began in 1896, when a cyclist died from a drug overdose. In the 1904 Olympics in St. Louis, marathon runner Thomas Hicks drank brandy with the poison strychnine and won—but nearly died. Heroin, cocaine and caffeine were used widely until new drugs became available in the 1930s. In the 1950s, the Soviet Olympic team used male hormones for strength and power, and the American team developed steroids.

However, Olympic cheating began in ancient times. Callipateira was the daughter, sister and mother of Olympic athletes. As married women were not allowed to watch the games, she dressed like a coach. A rule was then introduced that all coaches must strip to make sure they were men.

(313 words)

Language note

The word *conquer* used in the Olympic Creed has a meaning of defeating an enemy. It's not perfectly appropriate to modern sport, but has its roots in war, as do many of the Olympic events.

Vocabulary notes

1. **creed** (noun) a set of beliefs or principles, especially someone's religious or political beliefs
2. **opponent** (noun) someone who tries to defeat another person in a competition, game, etc.
3. **prohibit** (verb) to have a law or rule that stops people doing something
4. **score** (verb) to win points in a game or competition
5. **strip** (verb) to take off your clothes
6. **struggle** (noun) when someone tries hard for a long time to achieve something
7. **trick** (noun) something you do in order to deceive someone
8. **triumph** (noun) an important success or victory, especially after a difficult struggle

Read and listen again to practice your pronunciation.

The Olympic Games

After you read

A. Summarize the main idea in one sentence.

In 1964, at the first Olympic judo event in Tokyo, seventy-four participants from twenty-seven countries competed. Judo was included at the request of the Japanese hosts of the games. They were considered the best at this sport and perhaps thought they would easily win a lot of medals but were greatly surprised when Dutchman Anton Geesink won the open class event!

1964 first Olympic judo event in tokyo

Japanese interpreter photographs judo champion Anton Geesink, Tokyo 1964

B. Vocabulary check: Circle the words.

- ancient
- boxing
- chariot
- competed
- trick
- discus
- fence
- honor
- medal
- opponent
- score
- struggle
- wrestling
- sailing

Culture note

The modern Olympic Games have a lot in common with the ancient games: art, coaches, coins, fair play, rules, judges, music, oaths, parades and torches.

C. Choose the best answer.

1. The first Olympic Games were not based on __d__.
   a. festivals
   b. funerals
   c. births
   d. weddings

2. The early Olympics did not include __b__.
   a. races on foot and by chariot
   b. discus throwing, boxing and wrestling
   c. boxing, fencing and riding horses
   d. golf, tennis and sailing

3. The Christian Roman Emperor Theodosius stopped the Olympics because he didn't like __c__.
   a. worshipping religions apart from Christianity
   b. the Roman gods
   c. mixing sports and religion
   d. emperors participating in the Olympic Games

4. Which statement is not true? The first international Olympics ___.
   a. were held in 776 BC
   b. were held near Athens, Greece
   c. featured athletes from fourteen countries
   d. sometimes lasted months

5. The Olympic Creed can be summarized as: __c__
   a. Winning is everything.
   b. It's not about the journey, it's about the destination.
   c. It's not whether you win or lose, it's how you play the game.
   d. Don't be a sore loser.

6. It can be inferred that Pierre de Coubertin __c__.
   a. was a disorganized person who enjoyed art and music
   b. was Emperor of Athens in 1896
   c. was a key figure in the organization of the first international Olympics
   d. was an athlete who enjoyed golf, tennis and sailing

7. Examples of cheating in the Olympics do not include __c__.
   a. unfair judging
   b. illegal equipment
   c. prohibited drugs
   d. lost uniforms

8. The word *tricks* refers to __d__.
   a. choices of jokes
   b. ways to keep clean
   c. styles of magic
   d. methods of cheating

Exam strategy

When you study for an exam, make a list of all the things you find hard to remember. As you master each one, cross it off your list.

Debate

Take one side, add your own ideas and debate in pairs or groups.

For: **The Olympics is a true sign of our civilization.**

Points:
- The Olympics presents the world with opportunities for cooperation and competition.

- Everyone who tries to be an Olympic athlete is a winner.

- New Olympic sports, such as snowboarding, present opportunities for everyone to participate.

- <u>Olympics makes us happy</u>
- <u>Olympics brings new sport</u>
- <u>Olympics makes us proud</u>

Against: **The Olympics is not a good model for young people.**

Points:
- Drug abuse in the Olympics endangers competitors' health.

- Rich countries have the edge over poor countries.

- Many Olympic sports are based on war and fighting.

- _____
- _____
- _____

Debate strategy

When you debate, try to give a point of view or some background to your argument, especially when it is based on a principle, system or theory of some kind.

Say:
- "Based on the principle that all people are equal ... ."
- "As clearly shown in any democracy ... ."

More ideas to debate

"The price of success is hard work, dedication to the job at hand, and the determination that whether we win or lose, we have applied the best of ourselves to the task at hand."
Vince Lombardi (1913–1970) Sports coach

"You have to expect things of yourself before you can do them."
Michael Jordan (1963–) Basketball player

Learn more

There are many ancient and modern Olympic sports. Find an example of an Olympic sport that you are not familiar with. Learn something about its history and rules and report back to your class.

Look online

Check out the website at www.read-and-think.com for extra learning resources.

Add new words to your personal dictionary on page 146.

Reach for the Stars

Lesson One

Before you read

- What is the purpose of exploring space?
- Will people eventually live on other planets?

What is happening in this picture?

On Mars

Unit 3
Astronomy
Economics

Read about it

- What are the different parts of a letter?
- How formal or informal is this letter?

A New Home in the Stars

43 Pine Crescent
Hong Kong

November 18, 2005

Ms. Anna Chan
5 Editor
Asia Times
554 Queen's Road
Hong Kong

Dear Ms. Chan,

10 I want to bring your readers' attention to one of our city's finest features, the Museum of Science and Technology. When I was there recently, I saw two exhibits that made me realize what important issues are before us today.

The first exhibit I visited showed the history of evolution. In the
15 exhibition, we can clearly see how, millions of years ago, small creatures formed and with curiosity or courage, or both, left their homes in the sea and ventured onto land. From then, there were many steps over millions of years, but these small and important steps eventually led to the creatures becoming people.

Language note

The standard titles are *Mr.* and *Mrs.* for men and women, and *Ms.*, pronounced *"miz,"* for women who aren't married or don't want to be identified as married or not.

26

The second exhibition, on China's contributions to the exploration of space, showed a very similar story. In fact, today we are doing the same thing, but instead of leaving the oceans to <u>crawl</u> onto land, we are leaving the Earth and reaching for the stars. Despite what anyone says, the money the government is spending on space exploration programs is not a waste. Rather, it is a matter of survival for the human race. Space is our future.

There are several reasons why we should pay for space programs. The first is that soon the population of Earth will be too great to feed itself. Another reason is that people are naturally curious. We want to know about our universe and tools like the recently launched space telescope can help us learn more.

I urge everyone who has an interest in space exploration to visit the Museum of Science and Technology. The current exhibitions show both the history of human life and the future of space exploration, answering many questions about our place in the universe.

Yours sincerely,

Jodie Jensen

Jodie Jensen

(306 words)

Reading strategy

An important reading strategy is rereading, looking again at a passage but in a different way. You might skim a passage quickly on the first reading, looking for the main ideas and then read it more slowly, looking for supporting evidence.

Vocabulary notes

1. **curious** (adjective) wanting to know or learn about something
2. **current** (adjective) happening or existing at the present time
3. **exhibition** (noun) a public show where people can go and see paintings, photographs, etc.
4. **exploration** (noun) travel through an unfamiliar area to find out what it is like
5. **launch** (verb) to send a spacecraft into the sky or to put a boat into the water
6. **telescope** (noun) a piece of equipment like a tube, that makes things that are far away seem closer and larger
7. **venture** (verb) to go somewhere or do something new that may involve risks because you are not sure what will happen

Add new words to your personal dictionary on page 146.

Read and listen again to practice your pronunciation.

After you read

A. Answer these questions.

1. What action does the writer of the letter want to happen?
2. What two examples does she give to support her view?
3. Is the exhibition temporary or permanent?
4. What does she compare to exploring space?
5. Why might she say "is not a waste" in lines 24–25?

Understand what you read

Reading letters

Letters are either informal or formal. Informal letters include personal letters of thanks and congratulations. Formal letters include ones written for legal purposes or to and between companies. Formal letters are often considered contracts. For example, if you wrote to a store and asked them to send you a number of CDs, your letter would become a contract.

Letters are structured in similar ways. At the top is a return address, on the next level is the date followed by the name, position and address of the person you're writing to. A salutation, usually *Dear ...* with the person's title and family name is next. Sometimes there is a subject line, giving the purpose or problem of the letter, but this purpose instead could be included in the introductory paragraph. The body is the middle of the letter and includes arguments and examples, and is followed by a closing paragraph that usually suggests some kind of action. A complimentary close such as *Yours sincerely,* is next, then a signature and the name of the writer.

Here are four tips for working with formal letters:
- Quickly scan the introductory and closing paragraph(s) to get an idea of what the letter is about.
- Look for examples in the middle paragraph(s). Are they convincing?
- Guess the writer's attitude based on his or her language choices. Is the writer angry, amused, fed up, pleased or something else?
- Make notes on letters as you read them so you can remember what you first thought when you refer to them later.

> **Computer note**
>
> When you write letters, make use of the templates included in your word processing program. These templates provide spaces for you to include the main features of a formal letter.

B. Write the section each phrase comes from.

1. Dear Dr. Wong, _____
2. Finally, we would like you to fix the computer immediately or refund us our money. _____
3. For example, the telescope we ordered was black, but the replacement was white. _____
4. January 13, 2005 _____
5. I am writing to complain about the new museum hours.
_____

> **Language note**
>
> Dates can be written in different ways. In some countries, the month is written before the day, but elsewhere, it's the opposite. Dates written as numbers can be confusing: *1/12/2005* could be *January 12* or *December 1*. Write it out to avoid confusion.

C. Fill in the missing words. Use the correct form of the word.

> - **buffet** (verb) if wind, rain, or the sea buffets something, it hits it with a lot of force
> - **dilemma** (noun) a situation in which you have to make a difficult choice between two possible actions
> - **exchange** (verb) to give something to someone who gives you something else
> - **frontier** (noun) the limits of what is known about something
> - **massive** (adjective) very big or causing a lot of damage
> - **noble** (adjective) morally good or generous

Half the _____ of going to Mars is coming back. A _____ quantity of fuel would be needed for a two-way space voyage. But is it essential? Wouldn't you be willing to become a pioneer on the ultimate _____ even if you knew you would never see Earth again? You wouldn't be able to phone home; messages would be delayed ten to twenty-five minutes. But if you planned to make the _____ choice and stay, the fuel could be _____ for better shelter—and you would need it; the surface of Mars is _____ by 300 kilometer per hour winds and has an average temperature of -63°C!

What other problems do you think there might be in moving to Mars?

What about you?
You have just heard you are leaving Earth and moving to Mars. But you will never be able to return. You'll have all your basic living supplies and a computer. What else would you want to take with you? You have a box that is one meter by one meter. What would you put in it?

Lesson Two

Read about it

- How does this letter differ from the letter in Lesson One?
- What point of view does the letter writer have?

Why Explore the Universe?

November 23

Dear Francis,

Last weekend, I went to see a couple of exhibitions at the Museum of Science and Technology. The first was about evolution ... you know, ugly fish crawling out of the water and a few million years later they're all monkeys and then people. I know it's probably true, but the museum didn't explain it very well. It looked like you might walk along the beach tomorrow and see a fish turning into a monkey. I wish they had some pictures of what people might look like in another couple of million years. Maybe we'll start looking like fish again.

Then I went to the other exhibition. This one was about space. It was great but, afterward, I had some reservations.

It starts with examples of how early societies looked at the night skies and imagined all sorts of gods and <u>outlandish</u> creatures. Chinese fireworks were examples of early rockets. The first telescopes were next. I always thought they were invented by Galileo, but that's not true. It turns out that Galileo was just the first to use a telescope to study the moon and planets. There were lots of other important people, but I can't remember their names. The next big section was all about

Reading strategy

To understand and remember more of what you read, always ask yourself questions. What is the most important point? What is the least important? What facts support the points?

20 the rocket pioneers like Goddard and Von Braun. And then, finally, there was something on contemporary space exploration. This was all about men on the moon and different planned trips to Mars.

One of the things that bothered me was the fact that so few women were involved. I also wondered why so much time is wasted 25 exploring space when we're still ignorant about much of the Earth. For example, most of our oceans haven't been properly explored.

I guess space exploration is just more exciting for scientists.

See you soon,

Emily

(302 words)

Culture note

Astronomy, the study of the stars and planets, evolved from *astrology*. Astronomy is a science and astrology is a system of beliefs. Astrologists believe stars and planets affect the lives of people. Do you believe the stars guide your life?

Vocabulary notes

1. **bother** (verb) to make someone feel slightly worried, upset or concerned
2. **contemporary** (adjective) belonging to the present time
3. **ignorant** (adjective) not knowing facts or information that you should know
4. **outlandish** (adjective) strange and unusual
5. **pioneer** (noun) one of the first people to do something that other people will continue to develop
6. **reservation** (noun) a feeling of doubt because you do not completely agree with a plan, idea, etc.

Read and listen again to practice your pronunciation.

Reach for the Stars

After you read

A. Summarize the main idea in one sentence.

Around the world, many people starve and are without proper drinking water, shelter or education. The exploration of space is a noble pursuit but are we foolishly ignoring more important things on Earth? For the cost of a single space launch, quite a few hospitals could be built.

_____

B. Vocabulary check: Use the clues to fill in the crossword.

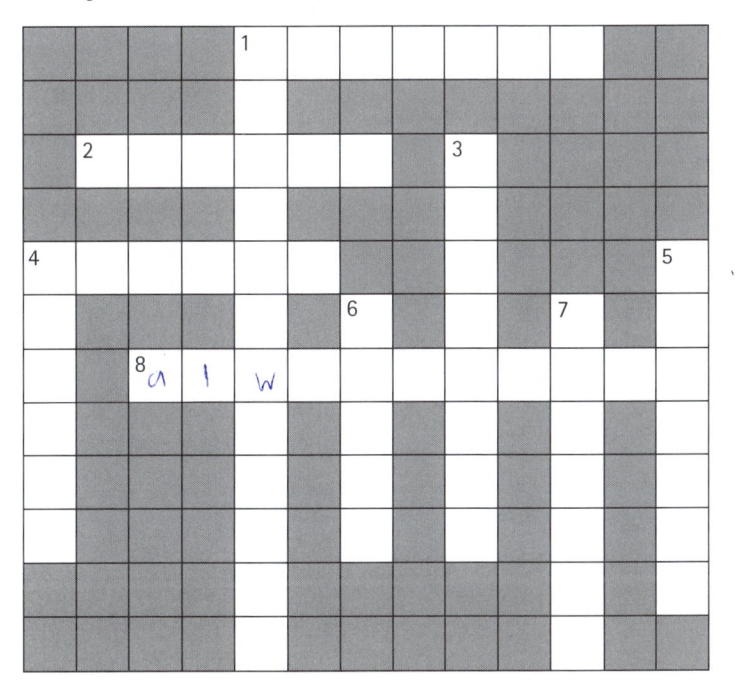

Across
1. always wants to know something
2. to send off into the sky
4. hit with force
8. looking for something new

Down
1. at the same time
3. you give me something, I give you something
4. Don't _____ . It doesn't matter.
5. a synonym for *to go*
6. a synonym for *good*
7. the first one to do something

Language note

Possessive pronouns and possessive adjectives don't have apostrophes. The contraction *it's* means *it is*. The possessive pronoun is *its*.

33

C. Choose the best answer.

1. Which is not an informal letter?
   a. A letter of thanks for flowers
   b. A letter of congratulations for a promotion
   c. A letter of request for a product
   d. A letter of confirmation to attend a party

2. *I am writing to order five CDs* would appear in what section of a letter?
   a. Salutation
   b. Subject line
   c. Introductory paragraph
   d. Complimentary close

3. The first letter suggests that ___ .
   a. just as we once ventured onto land, we are venturing into space
   b. we will eventually become something else beyond human when we go into space
   c. we are not leaving home again
   d. we are not happy on Earth

4. The purpose of the first letter is to ___ .
   a. inform Ms. Chan of how people developed
   b. discourage the government from investing in space programs
   c. advertise the new space telescope
   d. encourage people to support space exploration

5. In the first letter, what is not a reason to invest in space programs?
   a. The population of Earth will soon be too great to feed itself.
   b. People are naturally curious.
   c. It's a matter of survival for the human race.
   d. The environment is getting more polluted.

6. In the second letter, which is not a reservation of Emily about her visit to the museum?
   a. There were few women represented in the exhibition.
   b. We don't know much about Earth, let alone space.
   c. Other places to explore aren't as attractive as space.
   d. There was a lot of emphasis on rockets.

7. *Chinese fireworks* refers to ___ .
   a. an example of early rockets
   b. a type of outlandish creature
   c. a name of a planned trip to Mars
   d. a kind of telescope

8. Galileo ___ .
   a. pioneered fireworks
   b. imagined gods in the night skies
   c. studied the moon and stars
   d. explored contemporary space

Exam strategy

When you answer true and false questions, don't just look for the key words; read every word carefully. Sometimes an answer changes the meaning with a negative word, such as *not*.

Debate

Take one side, add your own ideas and debate in pairs or groups.

For: Everyone should support space exploration.

Points:
- Exploration is a natural human desire; space, the final frontier, is the place most worth exploring.

- Cars, trains and planes are recent inventions. Space travel will also be common one day.

- Our planet cannot support people forever. We must look for new homes.

- _____

- _____

- _____

Against: Space exploration is a waste of time and money.

Points:
- Most "space exploration" is really just a race for military advantages.

- There are too many problems on Earth to waste money on space toys.

- Travel to other worlds will not solve Earth's problems.

- _____

- _____

- _____

Debate strategy

When you debate, try to trap your opponents by thinking in advance about their arguments. Before they have a chance to explain their points, briefly say them, and explain what is wrong with each one.

Say:
- "My opponent will probably try to tell you that … but, it's obvious that … ."
- "I hope you are not going to try to suggest that … . It's a foolish argument because … ."

Another idea to debate

Humans may some day leave Earth and travel to other planets but it won't be cheap. Right now, it costs about U.S.$20,000 per kilogram to send something or someone into space. The dilemma of a mission to another planet would not only be the cost of sending enough fuel, but also enough food and water for a very long voyage. A few humans may some day go to other planets, but it won't be a practical way to solve Earth's problems.

Learn more

New efforts to explore space are being made all the time. What are the latest news items about space exploration? Find examples and report them to your class.

Look online

Check out the website at www.read-and-think.com for extra learning resources.

Add new words to your personal dictionary on page 146.

The Lord of the Rings

Lesson One

Before you read

- Who was John Ronald Reuel Tolkien?
- What is a metaphor?

Do you recognize anyone in this picture?

An actor and his character from *The Lord of the Rings*

UNIT 4

Literature
Biography
Fantasy

Read about it

- What is the story (the plot) of the novels?
- What are the names of the different groups?

Metaphors in *The Lord of the Rings*

J.R.R. Tolkien's *The Lord of the Rings* begins in a time before memory when twenty rings are forged that give the power to rule. Three are hidden by the kings of the elves. Seven are given to the lords of the dwarves and nine to the kings of men. But one other ring is created—
5 in secret—by the dark lord Sauron, to serve as a master ring to rule over all. That one ring is on his hand in the greatest battle in ancient times. But Sauron loses the battle and the ring passes to a man. When its evil leads to the man's death, the ring is lost. Then, it is found by someone

> **Language note**
>
> An *extended metaphor* is usually related to the theme, or message, of a novel. The theme of *The Lord of the Rings* is that even the smallest can help overcome great evil.

The English countryside, inspiration for the setting of *The Lord of the Rings* who becomes Gollum. In the novel *The Hobbit*, Gollum loses it and it is found by a hobbit, Bilbo Baggins.

Bilbo eventually entrusts the ring to his nephew, a boy by the name of Frodo Baggins. It becomes Frodo's quest to take it on a hazardous journey to Mordor to destroy it in the volcano where it was made. Along the way he is joined by friends—a fellowship of brave fighters who will help him—and together they encounter enemies. The task of returning the ring is made more difficult because the ring, as a metaphor for power, corrupts whoever wears it.

The Lord of the Rings novels are a metaphor for the struggle between good and evil, set in a mythical world called Middle Earth. Diverse people and monsters live there, each a metaphor for a different aspect of society; elves represent scientists and artists; wizards represent philosophers, whose ideas can be used for either good or evil; dwarves represent narrow-minded people, who live in dirt looking for wealth and are sometimes trapped in their own caves. Hobbits, the main characters of the three novels, live in a peaceful shire and are a metaphor for the simple life, ignorant of what goes on outside one's own home.

(325 words)

Vocabulary notes

1. **diverse** (adjective) very different from each other
2. **entrust** (verb) to make someone responsible for something
3. **hazardous** (adjective) something that may be dangerous or cause accidents
4. **metaphor** (noun) a way of describing something by comparing it to something else that has similar qualities, without using the words "like" or "as"
5. **mythical** (adjective) not real or true, but only imagined
6. **narrow-minded** (adjective) not willing to accept ideas that are new and different from your own
7. **represent** (verb) to be a sign for something

Add new words to your personal dictionary on page 146.

Read and listen again to practice your pronunciation.

Reading strategy

An important reading strategy is questioning. Question different points in a passage and keep a written or mental list of *who*, *what*, *when*, *where*, *why* and *how* questions to help you remember the main ideas.

Concepts

There are many made-up words in Tolkien's books. For example, a *hobbit* is defined as a little person, about half our height, who never wears shoes. Hobbits live in a *shire*, a word also used in England for a county, especially one in the countryside.

After you read

A. Answer these questions.

1. What is the main metaphor of *The Lord of the Rings*?
2. How did Tolkien represent different aspects of human nature?
3. What group does the author seem to admire most? Least?
4. Good novels feature great contrasts. What is the contrast in the plot of the *The Lord of the Rings*?
5. What does the author see as the bad side of the simple life?

Culture note

The Lord of the Rings is full of poetry. One of the most famous couplets is about the purpose of the ring that must be destroyed:
*One ring to rule them all,
One ring to find them,
One ring to bring them all and in the darkness bind them.*

Understand what you read

Looking at metaphors

A metaphor explains something that is unfamiliar by describing it as something that is familiar. For example, the expression, "Life is a journey." The idea of life is difficult to explain because it is so rich and varied. But a journey is easy to understand; you take journeys every day. Concepts such as death, dying and evil are often explained with metaphors. You probably use metaphors every day without thinking about them. If you eat something bad in a restaurant, you might cry out, "This is dog food!" You don't really mean it is dog food, you are just using a metaphor to make a comparison.

Here are four tips for working with metaphors:
- Metaphors are only useful when you understand the simple part of the comparison. In the example above, if you did not know what dog food was, the metaphor would not be helpful.
- Be aware of mixed metaphors: ideas which do not logically follow. For example, *His ideas were clouded in a sea of troubles*, doesn't make sense because seas are not usually clouded. It would be better to change *clouded* to *drowned* or *sea* to *fog*.
- Extended metaphors are metaphors that are carried across several sentences or lines of a poem or speech, or even an entire novel.
- When metaphors are used too often and become too familiar, they become clichés. When you come across clichés, try to think of how they could be said more interestingly.

Computer note

When you find interesting words and phrases on the WWW, add them to your personal dictionary. Start by making a file with the letters A to Z. Add new items alphabetically for later reference.

The Lord of the Rings

B. Explain the comparisons.

1. "I hear you are in hot water again," a friend told Charles Spurgeon. "I'm not the one in hot water," Spurgeon replied. "The other fellows are. I'm the man who makes the water boil."

2. When the young sculptor Constantin Brancusi (1876–1957) moved to Paris, he was invited by the famous sculptor Auguste Rodin (1814–1917) to work in his studio. Brancusi thanked him, but refused. "Nothing," he explained, "grows well in the shade of a big tree."

> **Language note**
>
> Some metaphors are so common that you are unlikely to notice them. They are called *dead metaphors*.

C. Match the two parts of the dead metaphors.

1. body
2. foot
3. head
4. leg
5. neck
6. point

a. in time
b. of a bottle
c. of a chair
d. of a hill
e. of the class
f. of work

Now write definitions for each of the phrases.

1. _____
2. _____
3. _____
4. _____
5. _____
6. _____

What about you?

Could you write a famous fantasy story? Try filling in the blanks:

Once there was a _____ that was attacking _____ . The reason was because it wanted to steal _____ . The bravest fighters tried their best but _____ . When _____ wanted to try, no one tried to stop him/her/it. Using _____ , the hero _____ the _____ and _____ . But that was not the end! Later … .

Lesson Two

Read about it

- What genre of writing is this?
- How would you describe Tolkien's childhood?

The Creator of Middle Earth

John Ronald Reuel Tolkien, better known as J.R.R. Tolkien, was born in 1892 in South Africa. His parents had moved there looking for a better job for Tolkien's father. Three years later, Tolkien's mother took him on a trip to England to visit family. While they were away, they received terrible news: young Tolkien's father had died.

Growing up without a father must have been difficult for Tolkien but, when he was only twelve years old, his mother also passed away. In 1908, when he was sixteen, he rented rooms in a house where several other lodgers lived. He fell in love with one of them, a young woman named Edith Bratt. The priest who was responsible for Tolkien after his mother's death was very angry and made him promise to stop seeing her. Tolkien followed his wishes but, as soon as he was old enough, he married her.

As a child, Tolkien was captivated by languages and made up pretend ones. He became very good at

J.R.R. Tolkien

Reading strategy

To understand the differences between facts and opinions when you read, look for the words and phrases for opinions such as *many people feel*, *it's commonly thought* and *most people agree*.

The Lord of the Rings

other languages and, in 1908, he went to Oxford University to study languages and literature.

In 1915, he joined the army to fight in World War I, or the Great War, as it was known until World War II. After months of waiting, he was dispatched to France and fought in battle against the Germans. During his short time in the army, he saw his best friends die. But he soon became too ill to fight and returned to England the following year. Around 1933, he began to recount for his children a fantasy story of a hobbit called Bilbo. He first put *The Hobbit* in writing in 1936. It was a surprising hit and the publisher asked Tolkien to write another. He did so and, in 1948, published the sequel, *The Lord of the Rings,* which was published in three volumes between 1954 and 1955. Tolkien died in 1973, aged eighty-one.

(319 words)

A World War I soldier and his horse use gas masks

The word *middangeard* is an ancient expression for our world between heaven and hell. The two lines translate as: *Hail Earendel, brightest of angels over Middle Earth sent to men.*

Concepts

Euphemisms are polite or humorous ways of talking about something unpleasant. There are many about death: *pass away, meet your maker, join the angels, final journey, give up the ghost, an awfully big adventure.*

Culture note

Tolkien was an expert on Old English, which is difficult for modern English speakers to read. In one old poem, he particularly liked this couplet:
*Eala Earendel engla beorhtast
Ofer middangeard monnum sended*
Can you guess what it means? The answer is below.

43

Vocabulary notes

1. **captivate** (verb) to attract and interest you very much
2. **fantasy** (adjective) something that is based on imagination and not facts
3. **lodger** (noun) someone who lives in someone else's house, paying rent
4. **recount** (verb) to tell a story or describe events

Read and listen again to practice your pronunciation.

After you read

A. Summarize the main idea in one sentence.

Peter Jackson (1961–), director of the three-part *The Lord of the Rings* movies enjoyed filming them in his native New Zealand. One day, Jackson was asked about returning to Hollywood. He replied using a metaphor to make a joke: "Why would I leave the Shire, to go to Mordor?"

___

B. Vocabulary check: Fill in the missing letters to find the secret word.

```
              M y t h i c a l
              e n t r u s t
        c a p t i v a t e
      f a n t a s y
          r e p r e s e n t
            h a z a r d o u s
        r e c o u n t
    l o d g e r
```

44

The Lord of the Rings

C. Choose the best answer.

1. Elves are a metaphor for __b__.
   a. scientists and artists
   b. philosophers
   c. narrow-minded people
   d. simple, ignorant people

2. Frodo was __c__ the task of looking after the ring.
   a. made by
   b. invented with
   c. entrusted with
   d. represented by

3. *The Lord of the Rings* is a metaphor for __b__.
   a. the relationships between different aspects of society
   b. the struggle between good and evil
   c. the appreciation of the simple life
   d. power and its ability to corrupt

4. Tolkien was born in __d__.
   a. England
   b. France
   c. Oxford
   d. South Africa

5. Tolkien may have named his mythical world Middle Earth because __d__.
   a. he read a poem about this place
   b. he wrote his book between childhood and old age
   c. it was the site of a WWI battle between England and France
   d. he wrote the book in the time of peace between WWI and WWII

6. Tolkien's mother *passed away* means: __a__
   a. she died
   b. she went on holiday
   c. she became ill
   d. she married again

7. Edith Bratt was __b__.
   a. a character in Tolkien's books
   b. Tolkien's wife
   c. Bilbo's mother
   d. Tolkien's best friend in the army

8. Tolkien met his wife __b__.
   a. on a trip to England
   b. in the house where he rented rooms
   c. in the army
   d. at Oxford when he was studying

9. Tolkien fought in: __d__
   a. the Battle of Middle Earth
   b. World War II
   c. the Battle of Oxford
   d. World War I

10. Tolkien was born in 1892 and __c__ in 1973.
    a. captivated
    b. sent to England
    c. died
    d. recounted

Exam strategy

In questions where you need to read a long passage, read the questions first so you know what you are looking for.

45

Debate

Take one side, add your own ideas and debate in pairs or groups.

For: A few people who believe in the right things can change the world.	*Against:* There is little most individuals can do to change the world.
Points:	*Points:*
• It's important for everyone to think past their day-to-day duties.	• Most people are too busy to worry about the larger issues in life.
• There are many leaders, such as Gandhi, who did great things simply by talking to other people.	• Young people have great ideals but lose them as they grow older.
• People can't rely on governments to make the right decisions.	• People who change the world, such as Hitler, often do so for the wrong reasons.
• _____	• *most people have the Idea*
• _____	• *to chage the world*
• _____	• *but they are afaid to do it*

Debate strategy

When you debate, use visual aids if they can help you make your point. Handouts, overhead transparencies and writing on a board are fine but make sure people are listening to you, not reading something. Make your point quickly and clearly, explaining what you are talking about.

Say:
- "I just want to draw your attention to an important point here ... ."
- "As the upper right-hand corner of the graph clearly shows ... ."

Another idea to debate

The story of *The Lord of the Rings* is essentially about power, for which the ring is a metaphor. Lord Acton (1834–1902) wrote in 1887, "Power tends to corrupt, and absolute power corrupts absolutely. Great men are almost always bad men."

Learn more

Tolkien wrote *The Hobbit* as the beginning of *The Lord of the Rings* story. Find the book in the library or read about it up on the WWW and report back to the class.

Look online

Check out the website at www.read-and-think.com for extra learning resources.

Add new words to your personal dictionary on page 146.

UNIT 5

**Environment
Economics
Sociology**

Small Is Beautiful

Lesson One

Before you read

- How do big businesses help and hurt people?
- Who was E.F. Schumacher?

What's happening in the picture?

Protester in Seattle, Washington, USA

Small Is Beautiful

Read about it

- How are periods and commas used to signal series, clauses and the ends of sentences?
- What is the opposite of a modern economist?

Buddhist Economics

When it was published in 1973, E.F. Schumacher's book, *Small Is Beautiful: Economics as if People Mattered*, made a lot of people think about the ways we make money, and what we use it for. Here is a quote taken from the book:

"[A modern economist] is used to measuring the 'standard of living' by the amount of annual consumption [i.e., spending money], assuming all the time that a man who consumes more is 'better off' than a man who consumes less. A Buddhist economist would consider this approach excessively irrational: since consumption is merely a means to human well-being, the aim should be to obtain the maximum of well-being with the minimum of consumption. ... The less toil there is, the more time and strength is left for artistic creativity. Modern economics, on the other hand, considers consumption to be the sole end and purpose of all economic activity."

The quote makes sense to a lot of people who are tired of always working harder to buy things that don't really make them feel a lot better. What do

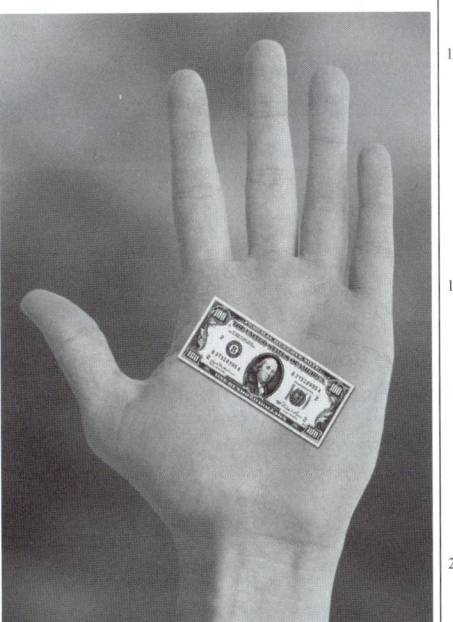

Decreasing value

Reading strategy

Sometimes you need specialized vocabulary when you read. To learn these words, read an encyclopedia article about the general subject area.

Language note

An *ellipsis* "..." is used to replace part of a quotation that is not necessary to understand the meaning of the quote.

people really want, and what do they really need?

Suppose someone decides that a bigger or better television would make life more enjoyable. Perhaps. But what does the person have to pay for that TV? It's not just the money, it's the lost hours spent earning that money.

Family watching TV

In any case, a family decides to buy a big television for the living room. But then the parents decide that they want a second television for their bedroom. What happens? They all can't watch both televisions at the same time. Perhaps one person in the family watches the one in the bedroom, while someone else watches the one in the living room. But then they are missing out on the happiness of being together as a family. There are lots of things we do that don't really improve our lives.

(318 words)

Vocabulary notes

1. **Buddhist** (adjective) relating to the belief and religion based on the teachings of Buddha
2. **excessively** (adverb) in a way that is too much or too great
3. **irrational** (adjective) not reasonable
4. **sole** (adjective) the sole person, thing, etc., is the only one
5. **standard of living** (noun) the amount of money that people have to spend, and how comfortable their life is
6. **toil** (verb) to work very hard for a long period of time
7. **well-being** (noun) a feeling of being comfortable, healthy and happy

Add new words to your personal dictionary on page 146.

Read and listen again to practice your pronunciation.

After you read

A. Answer these questions.

1. What is compared in the reading?
2. What is Schumacher's point of view on modern economics?
3. What might the title of the book, *Small Is Beautiful*, mean?
4. Why is "standard of living" in quotation marks?
5. Why is "better off" in quotation marks?

Understand what you read

Commas and periods

Commas and periods are the most common punctuation marks. Commas are most often used to separate items in a series including coordinate adjectives. Commas are used to separate a dependent clause that comes before an independent clause or to set off independent clauses joined by the conjunctions *and*, *but*, *for*, *nor*, *or*, *so* and *yet*.

Periods are used to signal the end of a sentence and are found after initials, many acronyms and abbreviations.

Here are four tips for working with commas and periods:
- Don't use commas to replace conjunctions in the joining of two or more independent clauses or when an independent clause is followed by a dependent clause.
- Don't use commas in place of semicolons. They have different purposes.
- American dates have a comma after the numbered date: April 1, 2006. Dates used elsewhere in the world often put the day before the month and do not have to have a comma: 1 April 2006.
- Commas and periods immediately follow the last letter of the word. Don't leave a space.

Computer note

The computer can sometimes help you with punctuation. In some word processing programs, errors are indicated by underlined sections. This indicates there may be a problem with the grammar, such as a sentence fragment. Always review these suggestions.

B. Add the correct punctuation.

1. The world's forests, mines and oceans won't last forever.
2. While the stock market is important, it's not the only measure of wealth.
3. Poor countries, especially in Africa, can't compete against developed nations.
4. E.F. Schumacher's book, "Small Is Beautiful," has made people think.
5. Progress, especially in the developed world, should not be paid for by the developing world.

C. Fill in the missing words. Use the correct form of the word.

- **aspect** (noun) one of the parts of a situation or subject that can be considered separately
- **private enterprise** (noun) the economic system in which businesses compete, and the government does not control industry
- **production** (noun) the process of making or growing things, or the amount that is produced
- **simplicity** (noun) the quality of being easy to do or understand, and not complicated
- **totality** (noun) the whole of something

"The strength of the idea of ___totality___ lies in its terrifying ___private enterprise___. It suggests that ___aspect___ of life can be reduced to one ___production___: profits. The businessman, as a private individual, may still be interested in other aspects of life—perhaps even in goodness, truth, and beauty—but as a businessman he concerns himself only with profits … private enterprise is not concerned with what it produces but only with what it gains from ___simplicity___."

E.F. Schumacher

What else is wrong with companies that just look for profit?

Language note

The term *Third World* has been replaced with *developing world*. Similarly, you no longer say *businessmen* unless it refers to a group of males; use *business people* instead.

What about you?

What problem in the world bothers you the most? What is something you could do about it? Make notes about a problem and think about creative solutions. For example, in the dry mountains of Chile, poor people did not have enough water. It was too expensive to buy water from elsewhere. But scientists saw that fog came each morning from the ocean. They built nets to catch water from the fog to give to the poor people.

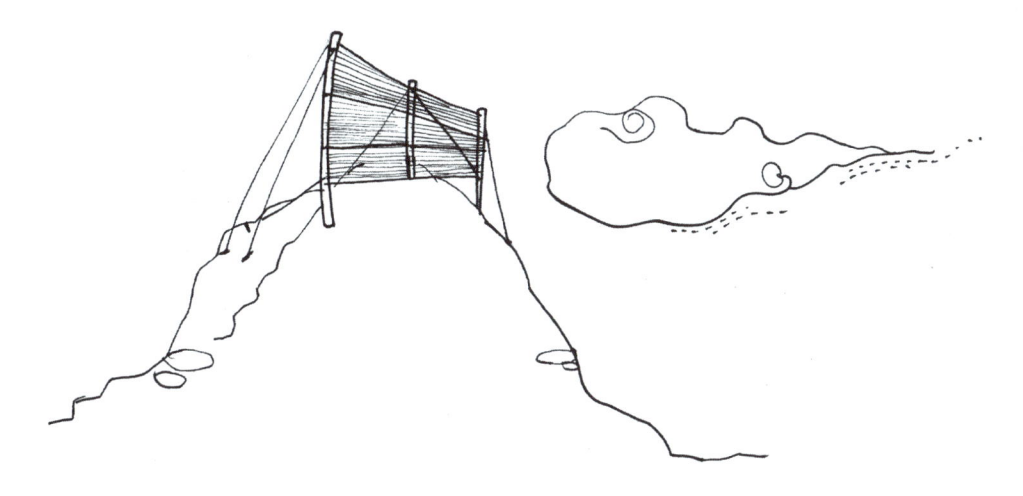

Lesson Two

Read about it

- What is the author's point of view on anti-globalization protests?
- What is the purpose of each of the paragraphs?

Anti-Globalization: Problems and Solutions

WTO Summit demonstration in Seattle

Language note

IMF: International Monetary Fund
WTO: World Trade Organization

On TV and in newspapers, you often see dramatic protests. Sometimes these are in the form of anti-globalization protests, especially at meetings of the IMF, the World Bank, the WTO or other large organizations. Modern activism is built around the idea that capitalism has gone too far. People feel that in search of profits, companies are robbing the world at the expense of the poor. Activists think that protests have become the only way to stop these companies,

Small Is Beautiful

as corporations control both politicians and international organizations.

These protests, with hundreds or even thousands of people, seem like a classic conflict between hero underdogs and villain capitalists. But it's actually more complicated.

Most anti-globalization activists are probably well-intentioned, that is, they think they are doing the right thing for the right reasons, but this does not mean they are always right. They generally see big businesses, governments and international agencies working together for the benefit of each other by cheating the poor. This might well be true. But at the same time, the protesters often ignore the good work that these groups do. Many of these organizations do a lot to make the world a better place. Meanwhile, the goals of the activists are sometimes vague and often unconstructive. For example, they are usually happy to protest against many things—pollution, deforestation and debt in the developing world—but they often don't really stand for anything. That is, they like to point out problems but they offer few solutions.

It's also ironic that anti-globalization protesters use global capitalist tools such as airplanes, cellphones and the Internet, to help them in their protests. During a protest a few years ago in the U.S. city of Seattle, Washington, protesters began smashing shop windows of the global coffee shop chain Starbucks. Then the same protesters ran in and pilfered all the coffee and carried away everything else they could steal. One protester, carrying armfuls of coffee bags, was asked what he was doing.

"Aren't you against companies like Starbucks?" the reporter asked.

"Oh, yes," the protester replied. "I am. But they make great coffee!"

When faced between global good and private greed, activists like this are as bad as the companies they criticize.

(369 words)

> **Vocabulary notes**
>
> 1. **activist** (noun) someone who works to achieve social or political change
> 2. **capitalism** (noun) an economic system in which business and industry is owned privately, and money is made from the profits of these
> 3. **dramatic** (adjective) sudden and surprising
> 4. **ironic** (adjective) an ironic situation is strange or amusing because what happens is completely different from what you expected
> 5. **pilfer** (verb) to steal a small amount of something, or things that are not worth much
> 6. **underdog** (noun) the person, team, etc., in a game or competition that is not expected to win
> 7. **well-intentioned** (adjective) well-meaning

Listen

Read and listen again to practice your pronunciation.

Discussion

After you read

A. Summarize the main idea in one sentence.

The following 1968 speech by anti-Nazi activist Martin Niemoller is often used to rally people to a cause.

"When Hitler attacked the Jews, I was not a Jew, therefore I was not concerned. And when Hitler attacked the Catholics, I was not a Catholic, and therefore, I was not concerned. And when Hitler attacked the unions and the industrialists, I was not a member of the unions and I was not concerned. Then Hitler attacked me and the Protestant church—and there was nobody left to be concerned."

Small Is Beautiful

B. **Vocabulary check: Use the clues to fill in the crossword.**

Down
1. _____ enterprise
2. to steal
4. to do something in a way that is too much
5. a follower of an Asian religion
7. to work hard or long hours

Across
3. serious
6. one part
8. an antonym of *complexity*
9. only one

C. Choose the best answer.

1. Schumacher thinks modern economic theories do not consider __b__.
   a. artistic creativity
   b. religion
   c. people's overall happiness
   d. people's standard of living

2. Which sentence best reflects a modern economist? __b__
   a. More is beautiful.
   b. Buy more, be happy.
   c. Whoever has the most, loses.
   d. It's all about shopping.

3. Which phrase best reflects a Buddhist economist? __a__
   a. Live for art
   b. Don't work
   c. More for less
   d. Trust in Buddha

4. A synonym for *toil* is __a__.
   a. work
   b. spending
   c. economic activity
   d. leisure time

5. A synonym for *activists* is __c__.
   a. heroes
   b. government
   c. protesters
   d. athletes

6. The phrase *global coffee shop chain Starbucks* means that __a__.
   a. the world should have more Starbucks coffee shops
   b. Starbucks coffee shops can be found around the world
   c. Starbucks has the best coffee in the world
   d. everyone in the world likes Starbucks coffee

7. The author of the second passage thinks that the problem with activists is that __a__.
   a. their goals are not helpful
   b. they appear often on TV and in newspapers
   c. they confront only half the equation
   d. they vandalize shops and steal things

8. *Hero underdogs and villain capitalists* refers to __c__.
   a. police versus criminals
   b. protesters versus big business
   c. business versus government
   d. protesters versus the environment

Exam strategy

Multiple choice questions are often written with two or more answers that are almost identical. Look for the differences.

Small Is Beautiful

Debate

Take one side, add your own ideas and debate in pairs or groups.

For: Globalization has helped make the world a better place.

Points:
- People may criticize globalization but they still enjoy its products and services.
- Many people who oppose globalization want poor people to stay that way.
- Poor people enjoy having international companies like McDonald's come to their countries.
- _____
- _____
- _____

Against: Globalization steals from the poor to help the rich.

Points:
- Businesses increasingly only invest in a country if the labor is cheaper than anywhere else.
- Globalization is making the world a boring place.
- Many businesses take developing world countries' natural resources and give little in return.
- Globalization makes some people only cares about money
- Globalization make rich people has more money left and poors has none
- _____

Debate strategy

When you finish a debate, add a conclusion in which you explain how you have proved or disproved the thesis, depending which side you are on.

Say:
- "Finally, it is clear, based on the facts I have presented (list them), that … ."
- "Although my opponent has tried to make you think that … my arguments (list them) have clearly proved that … ."

Another idea to debate

A survey in a 2000 edition of the French newspaper *Le Monde* showed 56 percent of people in France thought multinational corporations had benefited from globalization. But only 1 percent thought consumers and citizens had benefited.

Learn more

Globalization and anti-globalization protests are common topics in the news. Find examples and report them to your class.

Look online

Check out the website at www.read-and-think.com for extra learning resources.

Add new words to your personal dictionary on page 146.

Is Money Everything?

Lesson One

Before you read

- How important is money to you? What would you do if you had less?
- How would winning a lottery change your life?
- Can money buy happiness?

Check ✔ the diagram to indicate what you understand.

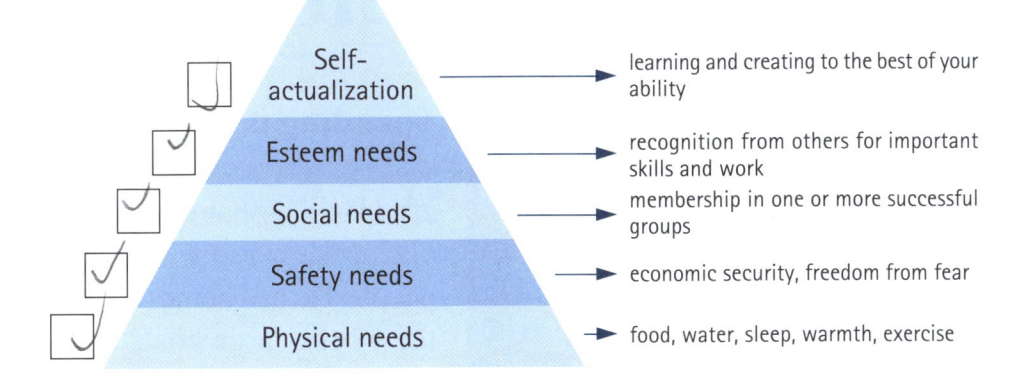

☐ Self-actualization	→ learning and creating to the best of your ability
✔ Esteem needs	→ recognition from others for important skills and work
✔ Social needs	→ membership in one or more successful groups
✔ Safety needs	→ economic security, freedom from fear
☐ Physical needs	→ food, water, sleep, warmth, exercise

Abraham Maslow (1908–1970) thought once people satisfy lower needs, they move to higher levels.

Label Maslow's level on each picture.

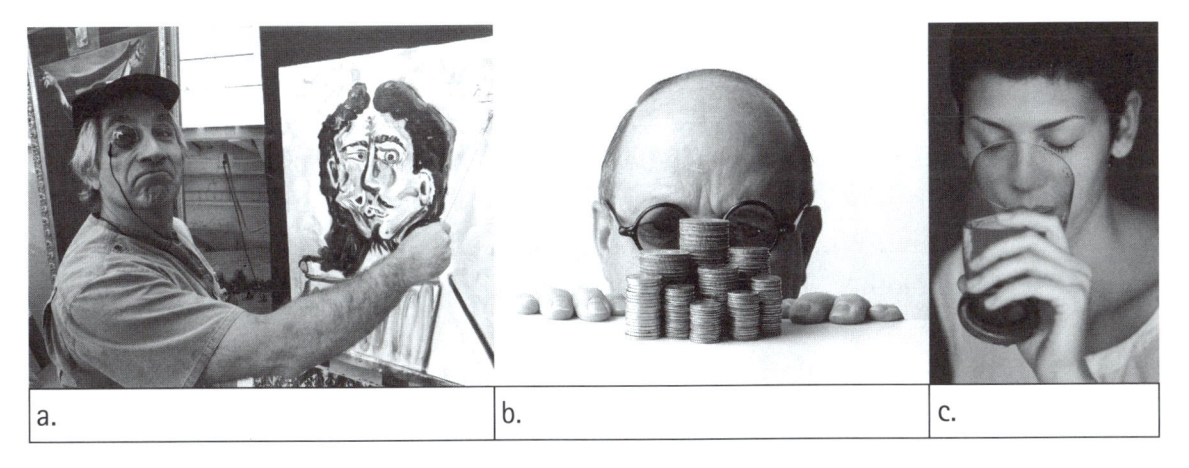

a.

b.

c.

UNIT 6
Philosophy
Psychology
Business

61

Read about it

- What do the title and subheadings mean?
- What is the article in favor of?

Healthy, Wealthy and Wise

Spending it

Adnan Khashoggi was once one of the world's wealthiest people. He had homes all over the world, large boats and a private jet. When asked how much he was worth, he laughed, "It's not how much money you *have*, it's how much you spend." The point he was trying to make was the importance of money is not how much of it you keep in a bank, but rather how you use it for enjoyment. It's a good attitude because when people do this, they spread their wealth to others. For example, Khashoggi's money pays for many people to work for him. When they have jobs, they spend money on things such as food and clothes. The people who make the food and clothes benefit, and so on.

Symbol of wealth: a private jet

The best in life

People have always pursued wealth. Money brings freedom to do what you want, live where you want and eat what you want. A poor person has

Reading strategy

To improve your reading comprehension, when you start studying a new subject, read as much as possible about it. For example, look for illustrated magazines and websites on the same subject.

fewer choices in life. If he or she can't afford a good education, then the choice of jobs is limited. In many cases, even when an education is available, it isn't possible because the poor person needs to work just to get enough to eat. A wealthy person can afford to take chances and improve himself or herself. A wealthy person also has better health care and education. A wealthy person's home is more comfortable and probably safer, too.

Creating wealth

Affluent people make others wealthy as well. Bill Gates is a good example. He has become the richest person in the world but his company has also made many other people millionaires. Countless people who now use computers have improved their incomes in smaller ways, doing work they couldn't do before and, often, doing it faster and more efficiently.

(300 words)

Bill Gates, founder of Microsoft

Vocabulary notes

1. **affluent** (adjective) rich
2. **countless** (adjective) very many
3. **income** (noun) the money that you earn
4. **pursue** (verb) to continue doing something, or to try to achieve something over a long period of time

Add new words to your personal dictionary on page 146.

Read and listen again to practice your pronunciation.

After you read

A. Answer these questions.

1. Who is Adnan Khashoggi?
2. What is important about having money?
3. How does Bill Gates help make other people wealthy?
4. Why have people always pursued money?
5. What does the title of this article mean?

Understand what you read

Survey

Surveying involves gathering information and thinking about your goals for reading. For example, is your goal to remember, or to use the information to answer questions? Depending on your goal, the way you read will be different.

Here are four tips for gathering information:
- Read the title. What does it tell you about what you are going to read? Often titles are humorous or give a surprising twist.
- Read the first sentence and think about the author's purpose in writing.
- Pay attention to unusual type, such as **bold**, *italics*, <u>underline</u> and information in "quotes." Look at subheadings and predict what you will read in the paragraph.
- Study graphics such as charts, diagrams, maps and photos.

Computer tips

<u>Underline</u> and ALL CAPS are from a time when people mostly used pens or typewriters to write. They add emphasis, but if you're using a computer, it's better to use *italics* or **bold**. Save "quotation marks" for direct speech or words that have unusual meanings.

B. Guess what each title is about.

1. Ten Steps to Financial Security
2. How I Lost a Million—and Found Happiness!
3. Gambling Is for Losers
4. Throw Away Your Credit Cards
5. Education Is the Best Use of Money

Is Money Everything?

C. **Fill in the missing words. Use the correct form of the word.**

- **measure** (noun) an amount of something good or something that you want, for example, success or freedom
- **prosperous** (adjective) successful and rich
- **source** (noun) the thing, place or person that you get something from
- **virtuous** (adjective) having a lot of money, possessions, etc., behaving in a very honest and moral way; opposite of wicked
- **wise** (adjective) a wise person is able to make good decisions and give good advice because they have had a lot of experience

"Today the greatest single _____ of wealth is between your ears."

Brian Tracy (1944–) Motivational speaker

"Early to bed, early to rise, makes a man healthy, wealthy and ___wise___."

Benjamin Franklin (1706–1790) American scientist, inventor, statesman and philosopher

"The real ___source___ of your wealth is how much you'd be worth if you lost all your money."

Unknown

"Being extremely ___virtuous___ and ___wise___ at the same time is impossible."

Plato (427–347 BC) Greek philosopher

What other sayings about money do you know?

What about you?
How much money did you spend last week? What did you spend it on? Make a list and circle the things you couldn't live without. Underline the things that made you happiest. Do you think you should change what you spend money on?

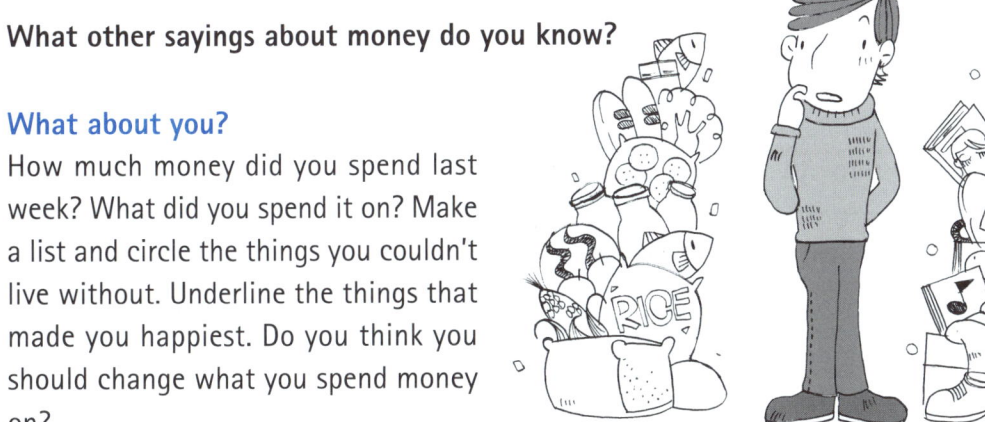

65

Lesson Two

Read about it

- What is the best way to measure wealth?
- Is it money that is important or the things that it buys?

Money Isn't Everything

Does money make people happier? Studies show that it *does*—when people at the poverty level are suddenly paid more. Other studies also show that people who *lose* the money they are used to having become very unhappy. But the most important thing seems to be that people are happiest when they make more than other people. Perhaps one secret of happiness is just to think about people who don't have as much money as you. Sadly, however, the opposite is also true. When you compare yourself to friends and neighbors who have greater incomes, you may become unhappy.

People in poverty need enough food to be healthy but what happens when people suddenly become prosperous? This is the case in China right now where people have become wealthy, but can only have one child. The result

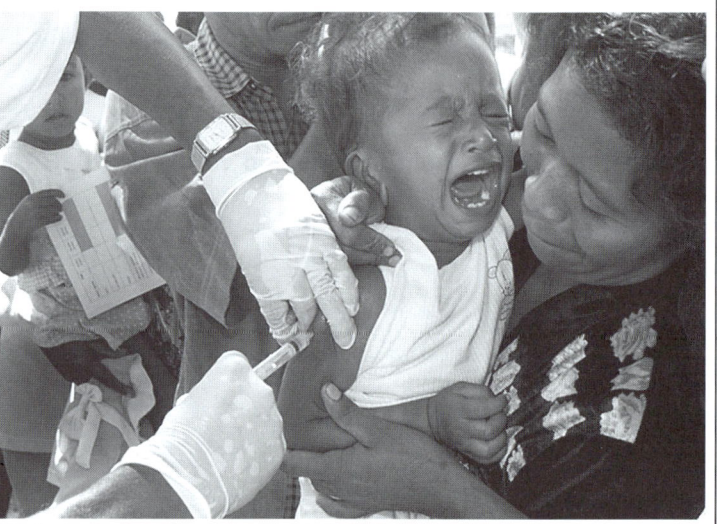

A baby immunized by a volunteer in East Timor

Reading strategy

Never be afraid to ask for help when you come across new words. A teacher, parent, librarian or friend can help you to improve your reading comprehension.

66

is an army of "little emperors": fat, spoiled children. A child measures happiness in love, not food, and there's nothing good about over-feeding a child.

Richard Layard, director of the London School of Economics, says, "The six key factors now scientifically established to affect happiness most are: mental health, satisfying and secure work, a secure and loving private life, a safe community, freedom, and moral values." It is quite interesting that only one of these has to do with making money. People who realize this think that it is better to be paid in something other than money, for example, time.

Many people are now starting to take time off in different ways. Rather than saving up their vacations for a rushed trip once a year, people are taking a day or so here and there to have smaller, quieter vacations. In some cases, people are going in the other direction and taking vacations of several months or even a year. On these vacations, they don't generally just lie on a beach. Instead, they might volunteer in another country or learn a new skill like a foreign language.

(323 words)

Vocabulary notes

1. **study** (noun) a piece of work that someone does to find out more about something
2. **poverty** (noun) when people have very little money
3. **secret** (noun) something that is kept hidden or that is known about by only a few people
4. **moral** (adjective) relating to the principles of what is right and wrong, and the difference between good and evil

Read and listen again to practice your pronunciation.

Concepts

There are different kinds of health. *Good physical health* means that we are strong, not sick. *Good mental health* means that our minds are not too troubled by problems. *Emotional health* is similar to mental health but refers to the way we deal with our problems and those of others.

After you read

A. Summarize the main idea in one sentence.

People's expectations increase with their incomes. Someone at the poverty level might be satisfied with one telephone, but wealthier people may "need" to have the latest cellphone. In 1980, no one had a cellphone. Now people complain when their cellphone cannot be used worldwide. People are never happy.

B. Vocabulary check: Circle the words.

B	C	O	U	N	T	L	E	S	S	H	E	W	X	E
B	E	W	S	A	S	B	R	E	A	I	E	I	D	T
S	V	I	R	T	U	O	U	S	O	N	S	S	I	A
E	S	D	B	N	S	B	E	T	M	C	E	E	D	M
C	P	U	R	S	U	E	Y	E	E	O	C	Z	L	E
R	P	S	E	M	S	S	S	E	L	M	H	Y	M	T
E	O	H	C	O	S	E	D	M	E	E	E	E	E	O
T	V	F	S	R	W	E	S	C	C	S	E	E	A	E
G	E	F	S	A	F	F	L	U	E	N	T	W	S	B
S	R	R	G	L	S	S	T	U	D	Y	C	I	U	A
B	T	A	E	U	A	E	G	E	E	E	A	S	R	S
J	Y	P	R	O	S	P	E	R	O	U	S	C	E	E
I	D	V	S	S	T	G	E	N	T	P	C	H	W	E
M	P	O	V	E	R	T	Y	Y	P	S	P	U	R	D

countless	income	secret	measure
wise	study	moral	prosperous
virtuous	poverty	pursue	affluent

Culture note

Money is important in religion in many parts of Asia. Is there a god of money in your culture? Is money used in any special ceremonies, such as weddings?

C. Choose the best answer.

1. Another title for the main passage in Lesson Two might be __b__ .
   a. *Throw Away Your Money*
   b. *Six Keys to Happiness*
   c. *Get Rich Quick*
   d. *How to Make More Money*

2. The passage is based on __b__ .
   a. newspaper reports
   b. studies by experts
   c. neighbors and friends
   d. unhappy people

3. Richard Layard __d__ .
   a. probably makes a lot of money
   b. studies people and money
   c. lives in London
   d. compares himself to friends and neighbors

4. People are happiest when __a__ .
   a. they make more than others
   b. they make less than others
   c. they meet others
   d. they work for others

5. The passage in Lesson Two suggests that __b__ .
   a. no one should try to become rich
   b. being wealthy is only good for rich people
   c. wealth isn't the most important thing in life
   d. poverty brings much happiness

6. The phrase *it is better to be paid in something other than money* means that __b__ .
   a. money is not important
   b. some things are more important than money
   c. we don't need money
   d. we need time to make more money

7. Which of the following is *not* one of Layord's six keys: __c__
   a. lots of friends
   b. mental health
   c. freedom
   d. moral values

8. A *"little emperor"* is __c__ .
   a. someone who lives in China
   b. a prince or other member of royalty
   c. a child in poverty
   d. a spoiled child

9. Sudden wealth can __a__ .
   a. create social problems
   b. make people only have one child
   c. lead to smaller emperors
   d. spoil grandparents

10. Comparing yourself to people with more money can make you __a, c__ .
    a. happier
    b. less generous
    c. unhappier
    d. work harder

Exam strategy

Before an exam, ask if you are allowed to make notes on the exam paper. If so, circle the key words in the questions and readings to help you remember.

Debate

Take one side, add your own ideas and debate in pairs or groups.

For: Making money is the best way of achieving dreams.	*Against:* Making money can get in the way of your dreams.
Points:	*Points:*
• Being wealthy means you have better medical care.	• Many people work their whole lives and then are too old to enjoy their money.
• You are safer if you have more money.	• More money often means more problems.
• People have always tried to make more money.	• Money is only a measure of success, not success itself.
• *You can do what every you want with money*	•
• *Money makes life go easyer*	•
• *You can have health*	•

Debate strategy

When you debate, avoid telling long stories to support your ideas. Instead, try to use short summaries that make your point quickly. Rely on the audience's background knowledge. If you think most will know a story, you can just give the general outline and the reason you are telling it.

Don't say:

- "Once upon a time, there was a tortoise and a hare. They decided to have a race. The hare ... ."

Say:

- "Everyone knows the story of the race of the tortoise and the hare. It's the same story here where someone who thinks he is very skilled does not use those skills intelligently and ... ."

Another idea to debate

Many people balance time and money. If you spend more time working, you get more money—but you lose time to enjoy it! How long would you like to go to university for so you could get a better job? Four years? Ten years? If you get a good job, how many weeks' holiday a year would you want to have so you could enjoy your money?

Learn more

How do advertisements link wealth and happiness? Find examples and report them to your class.

Look online

Check out the website at www.read-and-think.com for extra learning resources.

Add new words to your personal dictionary on page 146.

UNIT 7
**Paleontology
Geology**

What Killed the Dinosaurs?
Lesson One

Before you read

- When did the last dinosaurs live?
- How did the last dinosaurs die?

What's happening in this picture?

> **Language note**
>
> The word *dinosaur* comes from the Greek words *deinos* meaning terrible and *sauros* meaning lizard. Learning Greek and Latin roots can help you increase your vocabulary.

What Killed the Dinosaurs?

Read about it

- What words describe actions and things?
- Who was Mary Anning?

Where Did They Go?

For thousands of years, people have found unusual old bones called fossils. There have been many theories about these discoveries. Many people originally thought these were the remains of giant gods or monsters. It wasn't until the nineteenth century that fossils were identified as being the remains of dinosaurs. Part of the problem was that it was rare to find a complete fossilized skeleton so people could not imagine what a dinosaur looked like.

One of the first and most successful dinosaur hunters was a young English girl, named Mary Anning (1799–1847). When Mary was only twelve years old, she excavated the world's first Ichthyosaur, an ancient reptile that lived in the sea. Mary sold this and other fossils to scientists who used her work to become famous. These scientists included Sir Richard Owen (1804–1892), who invented the name *dinosaur*.

The last dinosaurs suddenly became extinct about 65 million years ago—but not because of people. Although many movies show people

Fossil beds with dinosaur remains are found all over the world. A researcher in Utah, USA, chip rock away from dinosaur bones.

Reading strategy

Before you start reading, always ask yourself what you need to learn when you read. This can help you read more quickly by focusing you on the most important parts of the passage.

battling vicious dinosaurs, people and dinosaurs are separated by 63 million years. The disappearance of dinosaurs remains a perennial fascination, and countless theories have arisen to explain it. These range from the unlikely (they all caught the same disease) to the bizarre (aliens ate them). Other theories are harder to dismiss. Some of the main ones have to do with mammals, parasites, insects and poisonous plants.

Small rat-like mammals lived at the same time as the last dinosaurs and may have aggressively eaten dinosaur eggs. If the dinosaurs could not produce healthy young, there would be no more dinosaurs. Alternatively, small parasites in the stomachs of dinosaurs may have made them sick. Insects, such as lice and flies, may have driven them mad—so mad that they could not look for food. Or was it poisonous plants? If such plants stopped herbivores from eating them, then carnivores would have starved, too. However, these theories don't explain why marine reptiles also died out.

Fossil dinosaur tracks in Oklahoma, USA

(323 words)

What Killed the Dinosaurs?

Vocabulary notes

1. **alternatively** (adverb) used to suggest an alternative to your first suggestion
2. **bizarre** (adjective) very unusual and strange
3. **carnivore** (noun) an animal that eats meat
4. **extinct** (adjective) a type of animal or plant that no longer exists
5. **herbivore** (noun) an animal that only eats plants
6. **lice** (noun) small insects that live on the skin and hair of animals and people
7. **mammal** (noun) a type of animal, such as a human, a dog or a whale, that drinks milk from its mother's body when it is young
8. **parasite** (noun) a plant or animal that lives on or in another plant or animal and gets food from it
9. **perennial** (adjective) happens often or continues for a long time
10. **reptile** (noun) an animal, such as a snake or lizard, whose blood changes temperature with the temperature around it

Add new words to your personal dictionary on page 146.

Read and listen again to practice your pronunciation.

After you read

A. Answer these questions.

1. How might dinosaurs have become extinct?
2. How many years separated dinosaurs and people?
3. What did carnivorous dinosaurs eat?
4. What kind of insects could have driven a dinosaur mad?
5. Why is the idea of aliens eating dinosaurs a bizarre theory?

Understand what you read

Adjectives and adverbs

Adjectives modify nouns and identify or quantify a noun or a pronoun. An adjective usually comes before the noun it modifies.

Adverbs modify verbs and describe *how* something is done. Adverbs can also modify adjectives, other adverbs, phrases and clauses. An adverb indicates manner (*badly*), time (*slowly*), frequency (*twice*), degree (*quite*) or place (*upstairs*) and answers questions such as *how*, *when*, *where* and *how much*. Many adverbs end in *-ly* and can be found in different places in a sentence.

Here are four tips for working with adjectives and adverbs:
- Not all words that end in *-ly* are adverbs.
- Adjectives include colors and numbers.
- Many adverbs of place can also be prepositions.
- Adverbs can modify adjectives, phrases, sentences and other adverbs.

Computer note

Use the thesaurus in your word processor to find synonyms of common adjectives and adverbs. It can make your writing more exciting.

B. Underline the adjectives and circle the adverbs.

1. The largest dinosaurs only ate vegetation.
2. Dinosaurs could have been green or pink; fossils don't show colors.
3. People searching hard for dinosaurs should look at their modern relatives: chickens.
4. Dinosaurs gradually evolved over millions of years into giant creatures.
5. The last dinosaurs quickly died together around the same time.

What else do you know about dinosaurs and dinosaur fossils?

C. Fill in the missing words. Use the correct form of the word.

- **comprehend** (verb) to understand something that is complicated or difficult
- **fossil** (noun) part of an animal or plant that lived thousands of years ago, or its shape, preserved in rock
- **imagine** (verb) to form a picture or idea in your mind about what something could be like
- **record** (noun) information about something that is written down so that it can be looked at in the future
- **scholar** (noun) someone who studies a subject and knows a lot about it

China is a country popular with dinosaur hunters. The first _____record_____ of a dinosaur bone was made around 300 BC, by a Chinese _____scholar_____ named Chang Qu, who lived in Wucheng, Sichuan. Chang found a dinosaur _____fossil_____. He could only _____imagine_____ it was a dragon bone. It wasn't until the 1850s, more than two thousand years later, that people began to _____comprehend_____ the great age of dinosaurs.

What about you?

If you knew a meteorite was coming and soon people on Earth would become extinct, what are some things you would like to do in your last month?

I'm definitely quitting my diet.

Lesson Two

Read about it

- What are the two main theories in this article?
- What are the consequences of each disaster?

An Explosive End?

Scientists are still looking for a theory to explain the death of the dinosaurs. Especially something that explains why it happened so quickly, over such a large area.

One of the theories is based on volcanic eruptions. The most dangerous eruption of modern times was in 1815. Mount Tambora, a volcano in Indonesia, shot out one hundred and fifty cubic kilometers of ash. Some of this ash went straight up for forty-three kilometers. The sun was partly blocked and the entire world cooled by as much as 3° C. A year after the eruption, parts of Europe and North America were so much colder, that it was known as the year without summer. Less sunlight reached the Earth and ash covering plants meant food crops could not grow. About ninety-two thousand people died, most from starvation.

Volcanoes can kill in other ways. They can produce gasses that choke people. Some volcanoes cause earthquakes and giant

---

Reading strategy

An important reading strategy is *clarifying*: trying to find out more about what you read. You might look for explanations from other sources as well as look up definitions in dictionaries.

What Killed the Dinosaurs?

tidal waves. Sometimes a volcano's lava and ash buries an entire city.

Volcanologists (scientists who study the eruptions of volcanoes) are specifically interested in the impact of ash blocking the sun and lowering global temperatures. They wonder how this might have affected dinosaurs worldwide—and how it might one day affect us. This happens not only from the volcano itself, but also from the smoke of the forest fires it starts. What would happen if there were thousands of major volcanic eruptions at the same time? The world would become colder and the air would become unbreathable. Dinosaurs and sea creatures would die. Was this how the dinosaurs died?

Another leading theory has to do with a large meteorite striking the Earth, sending up dust, and starting forest fires and tidal waves. Such a meteorite may even have started a chain of volcanic eruptions, causing incalculable damage. But whatever killed the dinosaurs, we still don't understand why some species, such as turtles and crocodiles, survived.

(320 words)

Vocabulary notes

1. **erupt** (noun) an act, process or instance of sending out smoke and fire into the sky
2. **incalculable** (adjective) too great to be measured
3. **lava** (noun) hot melted rock that flows from a volcano
4. **meteorite** (noun) a small meteor that has landed on the Earth's surface
5. **specifically** (adverb) in a detailed or exact way

Read and listen again to practice your pronunciation.

After you read

Language note

Decades—periods of ten years—are often used in descriptions of events. A possessive apostrophe isn't necessary: *He was born in the 1980s.* (Not *1980's*).

A. Summarize the main idea in one sentence.

In the 1980s, Luis and Walter Alvarez discovered a layer of iridium dust in rocks in Italy. The iridium layer fell around the time of the death of the last dinosaur. Uncommon on Earth, iridium is often found in meteorites. The Alvarezes believe a large meteorite, kilometers in diameter, hit the Earth sending ash and tidal waves all around the world as well as starting forest fires.

Meteor Crater, Arizona, USA

B. Vocabulary check: Fill in the missing letters to find the secret word.

```
        c o m p r e h e n d
          r e c o r d
        a l t e r n a t i v e l y
            i r u p t
      s c h o l a r
            r e p t i l e
          l e c e
          e x t i n c t
    p a r a s i t e
```

Culture note

Throughout Asia, dinosaur fossils were once ground up and used as medicine. People didn't know they were eating dinosaurs!

C. Choose the best answer.

1. What is the most unlikely theory for dinosaurs becoming extinct?
   a. They all caught the same disease. *(a)*
   b. Rat-like mammals ate their eggs.
   c. Small parasites made them sick.
   d. Aliens ate them.

2. People did not kill the dinosaurs, because ___. *(b)*
   a. people were fascinated with dinosaurs
   b. people were battling dinosaurs
   c. dinosaurs were bigger
   d. they didn't live at the same time

3. In line 49 of *Where Did They Go?*, it can be inferred that ___. *(c)*
   a. herbivores ate carnivores
   b. carnivores ate herbivores
   c. herbivores and carnivores ate poisonous plants
   d. plants stopped carnivores from eating

4. A synonym for *alternatively* is ___. *(b)*
   a. secondly
   b. contradictorily
   c. on the other hand
   d. whereas

5. The eruption of Mount Tambora affected ___. *(a)*
   a. Indonesia
   b. the whole world
   c. North America
   d. Europe

6. Volcanologists do not study ___. *(d)*
   a. why dinosaurs and marine creatures died
   b. the eruptions of volcanoes
   c. impact of ash blocking the sun
   d. lowering temperatures from forest fires

7. Thousands of major volcanic eruptions occurring at the same time would not have made ___. *(a)*
   a. the world become warmer
   b. meteorites add to the damage
   c. the air unbreathable
   d. dinosaurs die

8. A major meteorite striking the world would not ___. *(d)*
   a. send dust up into the air
   b. lower global temperatures
   c. make the dinosaurs extinct
   d. decrease the number of volcanoes

Exam strategy

Always come prepared to an exam with extra pencils, pens and erasers. Don't spend a long time carefully using correction fluid. Most teachers only care about your answers, so just cross out your mistakes and move on.

Debate

Take one side, add your own ideas and debate in pairs or groups.

For: The same thing that killed the dinosaurs could kill us.	*Against:* Unlike the dinosaurs, we're able to think of ways to save ourselves.
Points:	*Points:*
• There would be no way to stop a chain of volcanic eruptions.	• Massive climate change would be predicted and prepared for.
• A meteorite collision may not be easy to predict or stop.	• Underground shelters would ensure at least some people would survive to start again.
• We now depend on getting our food and water from great distances; supply lines would be cut.	• We could blow up meteorites before they strike the Earth.
• _____	• _____
• _____	• _____
• _____	• _____

Debate strategy

When you debate, use notes but don't write out every word of your presentation beforehand. Even if you memorize your speech, you will sound artificial. Make it easy on yourself by writing down numbered points and referring to them, for example, 1. climate change, 2. shelters, 3. meteorites.

Say:
- "I would like to make three points. My first point is that we would be able to predict massive climate change. My second point is that we would be able to prepare for it by building shelters. My third point is ... ."

Another idea to debate

People are used to thinking of dinosaurs as stupid animals that could not survive. However, dinosaurs ruled the world for 180 million years, while people have only been here for 2 million years. And, unlike dinosaurs, we may kill ourselves with weapons of mass destruction. So, who is the stupid animal?

Learn more

There are many theories about the death of the dinosaurs. Find more about one of the theories mentioned in this unit or about a theory not mentioned and report back to your class.

Look online

Check out the website at www.read-and-think.com for extra learning resources.

Add new words to your personal dictionary on page 146.

UNIT 8

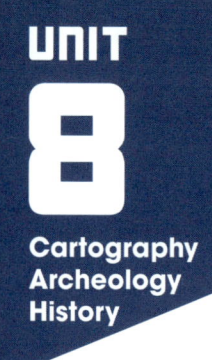

**Cartography
Archeology
History**

Looking for Lost Treasure!
Lesson One

Before you read

- Where are you most likely to find lost treasure?
- How do people lose treasure?

What is happening in the picture?

Photo tip

When you look at a picture, whether or not it has its own captions, make your own mental caption to describe the picture. It makes it easier to remember.

In the Aegean Sea, off the coast of Turkey

Read about it

- Listen for the different ways treasure has been found.

Lucky Accidents

On a cold January afternoon in 1943, a farmer, Gordon Butcher, was digging in a field when he found a big metal dish weighing almost nine kilograms. He told his boss, Sydney Ford, and together, they kept digging and eventually found thirty-four metal items in all. The metal was black, and a few pieces were bent. Ford stuffed them in a bag and took the items home. He left the bag in his cellar for awhile but eventually took the items out and displayed them in his living room. By chance, a visitor to his house recognized the pieces as Roman silver. It was the greatest accidental discovery of Roman treasure in England.

Terracotta soldiers from the tomb of Qin Shihuang, first emperor of China

In a similar accident, in 1947, a few young boys looking for a lost goat found a cave in the hills around the Dead Sea in the Middle East. In the cave they found clay pots filled with manuscripts. The boys sold them to an antiques dealer and the pots and their contents eventually found their way to Hebrew University. These Dead Sea Scrolls, almost two thousand years old, have caused the history of the Bible to be rewritten

Language note

The Dead Sea is a sea in the Middle East. Its name comes from its high salt content that means no fish or shellfish can live in it.

> **Concepts**
>
> People have often buried treasure for safety, especially in times of war. But sometimes they have not been able to return to find it. One "treasure" was the diary of Anne Frank, a young Dutch girl who kept notes during her time hiding from the Nazis during World War II. After she died during the war, Anne's father found her diary and published it; it is now one of the most widely read books in the world.

> **Reading strategy**
>
> It's easier to remember large numbers if you round them off. When you're making notes, you can give exact amounts (*4,722 pieces*) but you might more easily remember *more than 4,500* or *almost 5,000*.

and changed our understanding of early societies in the Middle East.

In 1974, a group of farmers in Xian, China, were digging a well when their drill disappeared into a hole. They had found a secret chamber. When the chamber was opened, it contained hundreds of clay warriors, the terracotta soldiers of China's first emperor. The soldiers are now on display and attract millions of tourists each year.

Not all accidental discoveries are made on land. In June 1993, Eduardo Gordevilla lost a fishing basket in the sea off the coast of the Philippines and dived into the water to look for it. Instead of the basket, he found something much more valuable: the remains of a Chinese trading ship that had hit a reef and sunk in 1414. On board was a treasure of 4,722 pieces that included Thai and Vietnamese ceramics, and Chinese gold coins. Almost all the items were in perfect condition.

None of these people were looking for treasure. They each just had lucky accidents—except Gordon Butcher. As the finder of the treasure, it should have belonged to him even if it was found on Ford's land where Butcher worked. Ford tricked him out of a fortune.

(392 words)

> **Vocabulary notes**
>
> 1. **ceramics** (noun) artistic objects made from clay
> 2. **chamber** (noun) a room used for a special purpose
> 3. **item** (noun) a single thing in a set, group or list
> 4. **manuscript** (noun) an old book written by hand before printing was invented
> 5. **reef** (noun) a line of sharp rocks or a raised area near the surface of the sea, often made of coral
> 6. **terracotta** (noun) hard red-brown baked clay

Add new words to your personal dictionary on page 146.

Read and listen again to practice your pronunciation.

Looking for Lost Treasure!

After you read

A. Answer these questions.

1. What treasures were discovered by accident?
2. Why might Ford have cheated Butcher?
3. How did the boys find the manuscripts?
4. What does the expression *found their way* mean?
5. What makes each of the different discoveries valuable?

Understand what you read

Phrasal verbs

Some English verbs have two parts made up of a verb followed by an adverb or a preposition (also called a particle). A phrasal verb has a different meaning than the verb on its own. The new meaning has to be memorized. Sometimes, a phrasal verb has two or more different meanings:
- Here is where the beach can *drop off* into deep ocean. (decline suddenly)
- I'm going to *drop off* if this movie is boring. (fall asleep)
- I have to *drop off* my bag at home. (deliver)

Here are four tips for working with phrasal verbs:
- Some particles can be separated from the verb and a noun or pronoun inserted. (e.g. *add* it *up*)
- Some particles can't be separated from the verb. (e.g. *get around the place*)
- Phrasal verbs often sound informal.
- There are single verb versions of many phrasal verbs. (e.g. *put out* a fire / *extinguish* a fire)

B. Add words such as *in*, *over*, *out* and *on* to make phrasal verbs and write the definition for each one.

1. come ___in___ means: _go inside_
2. take ___out___ means: _take something out_
3. work ___in___ means: _in work time_
4. march _____ means: _____
5. run ___out___ means: _run out_

Computer note

If you want to learn more about any of the stories in this or other units, just type key words from the passage into a search engine on the WWW.

Language note

Start a list of phrasal verbs and add to them as you read. Cross out old ones when you know them for certain.

C. Number these sentences in order.

___ Looking for them, the lake is searched but while no bodies are found, a muddy bag of dirty metal and glass is found.

___ The instructions lead Sherlock Holmes to an underground room where the butler has been trapped by the maid whom he pretended to love.

___ The maid is never found but at the end of the story, Holmes looks again at the bag's contents.

_1_ *The Musgrave Ritual* is a Sherlock Holmes detective story about lost treasure.

___ The only other clue to their disappearance is a ritual that turns out to be a set of instructions.

___ The story starts with the mysterious disappearance of a butler and a maid.

___ They turn out to be parts of an ancient crown of the Kings and Queens of England.

D. Fill in the missing words. Use the correct form of the word.

- **accidentally** (adverb) if you accidentally do something, you do it without intending to do it
- **metal detector** (noun) a machine used for finding metal buried under the ground, or one used at airports for finding metal weapons
- **rare** (adjective) very unusual or uncommon
- **settlement** (noun) a place where a group of people live
- **signal** (noun) a sound, action, or event that gives information or tells someone to do something

Not all treasure is found _accidentally_. In England, old coins are often found in places where there was once a _____. Fifteen-year-old John Philpotts had been looking for buried treasure since 1992. In 1996, he made a _____ and important discovery. Using a _____, he was searching a farmer's field when a _____ told him there was metal below. John found U.S.$100,000 worth of Roman coins.

Would you like to hunt for buried treasure? Why or why not?

Looking for Lost Treasure!

What about you?

Unless you are a scuba diver, you probably won't find underwater treasure, but there are lots of other treasures you could find from rare coins and stamps to unrecognized paintings by famous people. What other treasures might you find and where?

> Oh, good! I've been looking for those.

In 1966, a visitor at the National Library of Madrid found two of Leonardo da Vinci's lost notebooks.

Reading strategy

When you learn the names of countries and places, learn the adjectives that go with them, for example, *United States/American*, *Britain/British*, *Rome/Roman*.

Lesson Two

Read about it

- What is the mystery of Oak Island?
- How long have people been searching Oak Island?

The Mystery of Oak Island

In 1795, a teenage boy, Daniel McGinnis, was walking on Oak Island, Canada, when he noticed an odd tree over a hollow in the ground. He started digging and discovered a mystery. People are still trying to solve it today. Look at the timeline to see how the search has progressed.

- 1795: Daniel McGinnis and friends dig a pit ten meters down but then give up.
- 1803: A company helps the three friends begin excavation. They get down to thirty meters, but water floods in and they have to stop.
- 1804: This first company digs a parallel pit to thirty-six meters, but this also floods when they attempt to tunnel over to the original pit.
- 1849: A second company begins drilling. They drill through two wooden casks, or barrels, filled with loose metal. Some gold chain links are found.

Where might you find treasure?

Culture note

Many people refer to the pit on Oak Island as *a money pit*, an idiom that means something that consumes a lot of money but produces few benefits.

90

- 1850: A nearby beach is found to have a clever system of five hidden drains that fill the pit.
- 1861: A machine used to pump out water explodes. One man dies. After several tunnels into the pit are built, possible treasures at the thirty-six meter level fall farther down the pit.
- 1893: A third company begins investigating the pit.
- 1897: Stones with mysterious symbols are discovered. During drilling, a cement vault is found along with a piece of parchment with strange writing on it. Another man dies.
- 1899: One more secret tunnel, meant to flood the pit, is discovered.
- 1936: Another stone with mysterious writing is found.
- 1959: A fourth company begins work but four people die from poison gas in a tunnel.
- 1965: A fifth company uses big machines to dig a huge hole. Nothing is found.
- 1970: A sixth company takes over and lowers a camera down one of the pits. The camera sees human remains in the water. Legal problems delay exploration.

Why would anyone go to so much trouble to create the pit on Oak Island? Is there really buried treasure at the bottom? Will anyone ever find it?

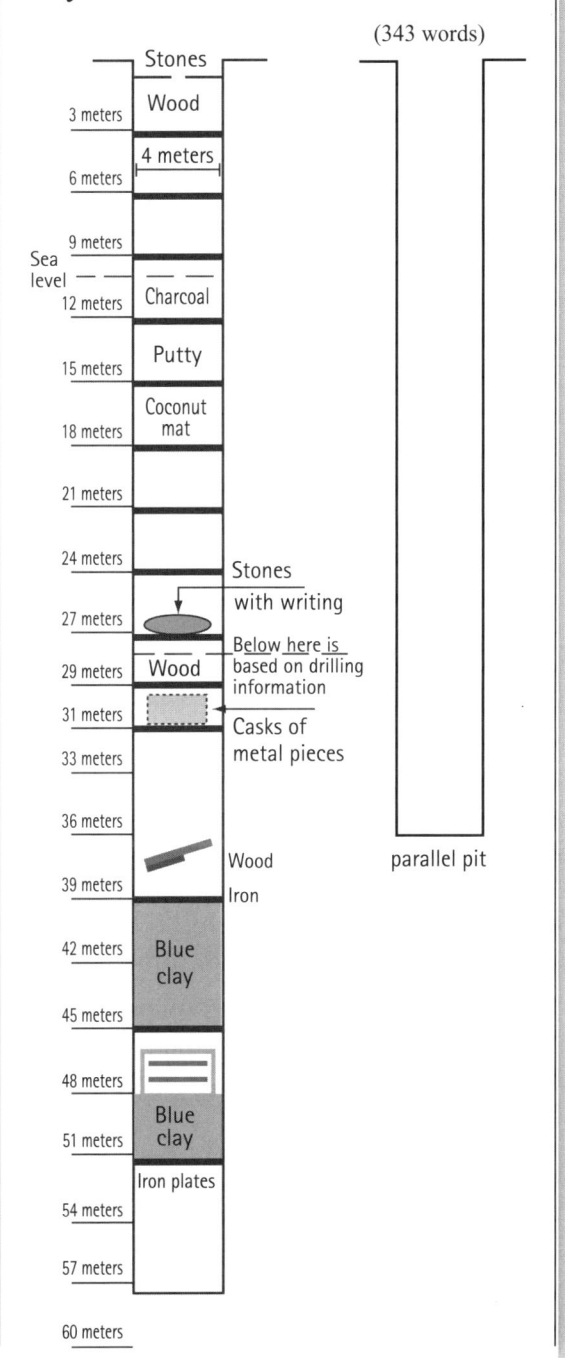

(343 words)

Vocabulary notes

1. **cask** (noun) a round wooden container used for holding wine
2. **charcoal** (noun) a black substance made of burned wood, used for burning as fuel or for drawing
3. **delay** (verb) to wait until a later time to do something
4. **drill** (verb) to make a hole in something using a drill
5. **hollow** (noun) an area that is lower than the surrounding surface
6. **mystery** (noun) something that is difficult to explain or understand
7. **parchment** (noun) thick yellow-white writing paper used in past times
8. **pit** (noun) a hole that has been dug in the ground
9. **solve** (verb) to find an answer to a problem
10. **vault** (noun) a room with thick walls and a strong door where money, jewels etc. are kept

Read and listen again to practice your pronunciation.

After you read

A. Summarize the main idea in one sentence.

Just before midnight on April 14, 1912, the ocean liner R.M.S. *Titanic* on her first voyage struck an iceberg and sank. In 1985, Dr. Robert Ballard and his crew found the ship in 3,810 meters of water. He could have made a great fortune by recovering the ship; some even proposed using balloons to float the entire ship to the surface to keep it in a museum. Rumors also say that great fortunes in gold and jewels are on board. But Dr. Ballard thought that it should stay where it was, remembering that it is also the grave of more than fifteen hundred people.

B. **Vocabulary check: Fill in the missing letters to find the secret word.**

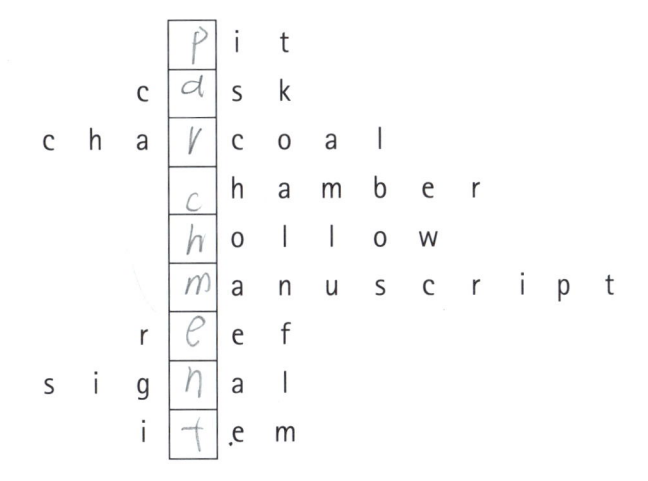

```
              p  i  t
           c  d  s  k
     c  h  a  r  c  o  a  l
              c  h  a  m  b  e  r
              h  o  l  l  o  w
              m  a  n  u  s  c  r  i  p  t
           r  e  e  f
     s  i  g  n  a  l
              i  t  e  m
```

Add new words to your personal dictionary on page 146.

Culture note

One person's garbage is another person's treasure. Archeologists learn a lot about past societies by looking through ancient garbage dumps.

C. **Choose the best answer.**

1. Oak Island is called a money pit because __d__ .
   a. there is now a bank machine there
   b. little money was spent for the many results
   c. few results were seen for the money spent
   d. the pit may be filled with money

2. People have been looking for treasure on Oak Island for about __b__ .
   a. 100 years
   b. 200 years
   c. 300 years
   d. 400 years

3. Oak Island's treasure has not been found because __a__ .
   a. of the difficulty of reaching the bottom of the pit
   b. pirates have stolen the treasure
   c. pirates have hidden the treasure elsewhere
   d. people have not been able to use modern drills

4. If you were going to look for treasure on Oak Island, __d__ .
   a. you would have legal difficulties
   b. you would need specialist equipment
   c. you would need a lot of money
   d. all of the above

Exam strategy

If you finish your exam early, use the time to go back and check your answers.

5. Treasure on Oak Island may never be found because __c__.
   a. there may not be any
   b. the map of the pit is missing
   c. too many people have died looking for it
   d. it has been already stolen

6. The diagram shows what the pit looks like from __b__.
   a. above
   b. below
   c. the side
   d. inside

7. Whoever built the pit must have had __d__.
   a. few brains
   b. twenty-first century tools
   c. few secrets to keep
   d. a clever plan

8. The treasure may have been found by now if only __a__.
   a. early diggers hadn't ruined parts of the pit
   b. people hadn't died
   c. the cave had been explored properly
   d. the pit was dug by hand

Face to face: Debate

Take one side, add your own ideas and debate in pairs or groups.

For: There are lots of treasures out there for people to find.
Points:
- There are many kinds of treasure.
- People are always losing things so there will always be something new to find.
- Many things are discovered that people did not know were lost.
- Anything left in the world could be a treasure
- There are still a lot of unknown treasure
- some treasure doesn't need equipment

Against: Only professional treasure hunters find the best treasure.
Points:
- Most treasure today is found using sophisticated equipment.
- Professional treasure hunters look at old maps and records to help them know where to look.
- There isn't that much treasure left.

Looking for Lost Treasure!

Debate strategy

When you debate, always try to speak loudly and clearly. When you are debating in front of an audience, instead of talking to your opponent, talk to the audience. In a formal debate, they are the ones who will decide who has the better argument.

Say:
- "Let me explain to all of you ... ."
- "I'd like each of you to understand that ... ."
- "I know you will all agree with me that ... ."

More ideas to debate

A stone was found at Oak Island with these markings. A language professor thinks he has broken the code. Later, however, the stone was lost so no one knows if it was real or a fake.

A = •	G =	M = ∓	S = ⊙	Y = ✓
B = †	H =	N = ✕	T = △	Z =
C =	I = ∴	O = ∙∖	U = +	
D = ▯	J =	P = ⊖	V =	
E = ⋮	K =	Q =	W = ▢	
F = ▽	L = ⌐	R = ⊘	X =	

Crossed out F = ⋈

Learn more

There are many treasure hunts on the WWW. Usually, they ask a list of obscure questions for you to research using key words to find websites with the answers. Find a WWW treasure hunt and report it to your class. You can also make your own WWW treasure hunt.

Look online

Check out the website at www.read-and-think.com for extra learning resources.

Add new words to your personal dictionary on page 146.

Language note

The code above is called a *substitution code*, because a symbol is substituted, or put in place, of each letter. Substitution codes often use numbers.

UNIT 9
**Military studies
History**

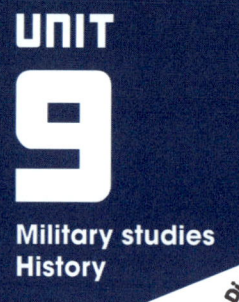

Into Battle!
Lesson One

Before you read

- What was the Battle of Agincourt?
- When did it take place, who fought and who won?

What weapons are the soldiers using to fight?

The Battle of Agincourt, from an engraving

Into Battle!

Read about it

- How was the battle fought?
- Which words are used to join phrases?

The Battle of Agincourt

One of the most famous battles of all time, the Battle of Agincourt, was fought on St. Crispian's Day, October 25, 1415, in Northern France. The battle was part of the Hundred Years' War, a series of conflicts between France and England that began in 1337 and ended in 1453.

This particular battle was between the army of King Henry V of England (1387–1422) and that of King Charles VI of France (1368–1422). Before the battle, before even the first arrow was shot, King Henry V gave a great speech that rallied his men to fight. This speech was adapted by William Shakespeare (1564–1616) for his play *Henry V*.

The battle is also remembered because the English, with many disadvantages, were able to defeat the French. The exhausted English had been marching and fighting for many days. When they arrived for the battle, the French had gathered a large force so the English army was outnumbered three to one. Yet, the English were able to

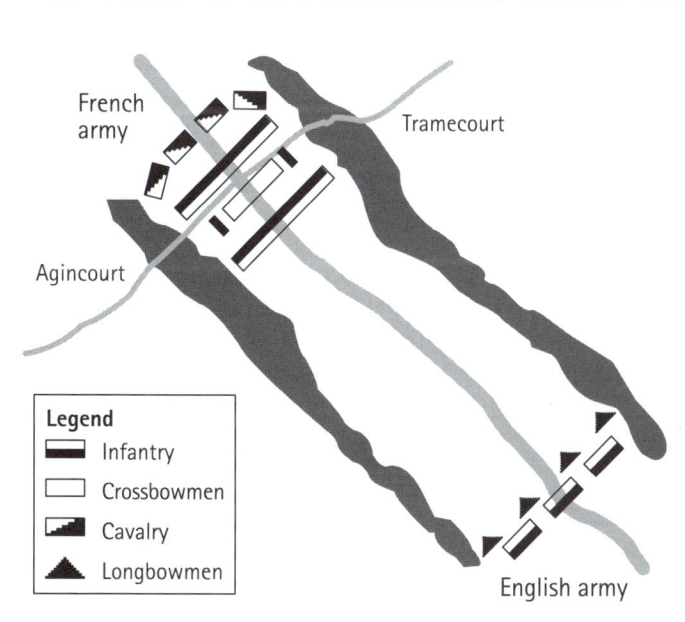

Language note

A *legend* uses symbols to help you understand a map or diagram. Always look at each symbol carefully and make sure you don't confuse two that look similar.

Reading strategy

Improve your reading comprehension by building your background knowledge before you read. Look at the headings, subheadings, charts, pictures and captions in the passage for clues to what it is about.

Legend:
- Infantry
- Crossbowmen
- Cavalry
- Longbowmen

> **Language note**
>
> Conjunctions such as *and* and *but* can begin a sentence. They often signal that the idea of the sentence is an afterthought.

have a great victory over the French on French soil. But although people like to think this was because the English were braver and fought harder, the battle was mostly won by mud.

At a farmer's field near Agincourt, where the two armies met, it had been raining for a few weeks. The earth had been plowed and the mud was deep. Neither army wanted to cross the field. The English held their position for four hours, waiting for the French to do something. Finally, when the French started sending their servants for lunch, the English shot arrows from their longbows which, as the name suggests, were able to shoot arrows long distances—much longer than the French army's bows. The French became angry and charged. Many French soldiers and their horses, all in armor, sank into the mud. Then the English shot arrows at the horses. The horses threw the French soldiers into the mud and they could not pull themselves out. Most soldiers drowned before they could fight or were easily killed by the more mobile English soldiers in bare feet.

(348 words)

Vocabulary notes

1. **adapt** (verb) to change something so that it is suitable for a new need or purpose
2. **armor** (noun) metal or leather clothing worn in past times by men in battle
3. **arrow** (noun) a thin straight weapon with a point at one end that you shoot from a bow
4. **bare** (adjective) not covered by clothes
5. **drown** (verb) to die by being under water too long, or to kill someone in this way
6. **exhausted** (adjective) extremely tired
7. **mobile** (adjective) able to move or be moved quickly and easily
8. **rally** (verb) to come together or bring people together to support an idea, a political party, etc.

Add new words to your personal dictionary on page 146.

Read and listen again to practice your pronunciation.

Into Battle!

After you read

A. Answer these questions.

1. Who was fighting?
2. The reading doesn't say why they fought; can you guess?
3. How did the English use strategy over the French?
4. Why was the French soldiers' armor not an advantage?
5. Why did King Henry V give a speech?

Understand what you read

Conjunctions

Conjunctions join parts of a sentence. The two main types of conjunctions are coordinating conjunctions and subordinating conjunctions. Coordinating conjunctions include *and*, *but*, *or*, *yet*, *for*, *nor* and *so*. When a coordinating conjunction connects two independent ideas or clauses, it is often (but not always) followed by a comma:

- *The weather was wet, but each of the armies was used to fighting in such conditions.*

When the two independent clauses connected by a coordinating conjunction are nicely balanced or brief, many writers will omit the comma:

- *The French had more soldiers but the English had better archers.*

A subordinating conjunction shows that the idea or clause that follows it depends on another clause in the sentence. Subordinating conjunctions include *after*, *because*, *before*, *even though* and *since*. Some subordinating conjunctions are also prepositions. Dependent clauses are separated by a comma if they come first, but the dependent clause may come before or after the independent clause.

- *Before the French would fight, the English had to shoot arrows at them.* (dependent clause first)
- *The English had to shoot arrows at them before the French would fight.* (dependent clause second)

Here are three tips for working with conjunctions:

- Decide if the clauses are independent (work as sentences on their own) or dependent (can't work as sentences on their own).
- Watch out for too many conjunctions in one sentence; it may be a run-on sentence.
- Conjunctions allow you to omit words.

Language note

To help remember coordinating conjunctions, use the acronym FANBOYS: For-And-Nor-But-Or-Yet-So.

B. Join the sentences with the conjunctions.

1. (or) Everyone had to fight. They would be captured.
2. (since) The English nobles weren't worried. They would be ransomed.
3. (but) The other soldiers might be taken as prisoners. They would be killed.
4. (and) Their jewels would be taken. Their bodies would be left to rot.
5. (before) King Henry V ordered all French prisoners killed. They could turn on the English.

C. Fill in the missing words. Use the correct form of the word.

- **captor** (noun) someone who keeps another person as a prisoner
- **combat** (noun) fighting during a war
- **jewelry** (noun) things that you wear for decoration, such as rings and necklaces
- **prisoner** (noun) someone who is forced to stay somewhere, for example during a war
- **ransom** (noun) the money paid to free someone who is being kept as a prisoner
- **scavenge** (verb) to search for food or things to use among unwanted food or objects

As the French began to lose, English soldiers seized prisoners for _ransom_ and _scavenge_ armor and _combat_ from the dead. However, the battle was not over and the remaining French still easily outnumbered the English. As French leaders tried to rally their troops for another attack, King Henry V gave the order to kill the _prisoner_. This removed the risk of them turning on their _captor_ and freed their guards for _jewelry_.

What other strategies do armies use in battle?

What about you?

If you were a leader could you write a speech to make people want to follow you? Try. Imagine your plane has crashed in the mountains. You want to lead the people down the mountain but some are afraid and just want to stay with the plane where they will freeze. Make a few notes for a short speech to convince everyone to join you.

Lesson Two

Read about it

- How does Shakespeare's English compare to English today?
- How does the speech use repetition to add emotion?

Band of Brothers

Shortly before the Battle of Agincourt, King Henry V called his soldiers together to deliver a speech. He knew that there were far more French soldiers than English soldiers. He also knew that the French were not as tired as his own soldiers, who had been traveling and fighting for some time. King Henry's speech was meant to give his soldiers the courage to fight and defeat the enemy.

William Shakespeare wrote a series of what are now called his historical plays. These mostly showed the great moments in English history. After the Battle of Agincourt, King Henry's speech was made famous in Shakespeare's 1599 play, *Henry V*. Because the fight is due to take place on St. Crispian's Day, King Henry tells his soldiers that the story will be taught to every boy and, on every anniversary of the battle, all the

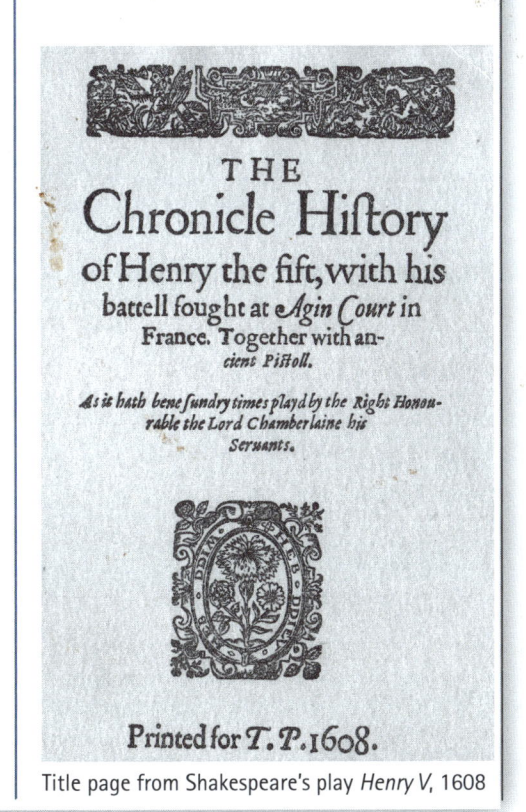

Title page from Shakespeare's play *Henry V*, 1608

soldiers who fought will be proud to show their scars.

Like much of Shakespeare's work, some of the English is difficult to understand. Shakespeare uses words such as *whiles* for *while*, and some words have unusual contractions, such as *ne'er* for *never* and *accurs'd* for *accursed*, to make them fit into the rhyme of the speech.

This story shall the good man teach his son;
And Crispin Crispian shall ne'er go by,
From this day to the ending of the world,
But we in it shall be remembered—
We few, we happy few, we band of brothers;
For he today that sheds his blood with me
Shall be my brother; be he ne'er so vile,
This day shall gentle his condition;
And gentlemen in England now a-bed
Shall think themselves accurs'd they were not here,
And hold their manhoods cheap whiles any speaks
That fought with us upon Saint Crispian's day.
(4.3.57–67)

Laurence Olivier in Henry V

Shakespeare was a playwright, not a historian, so he wrote his plays to be dramatic, even though they weren't always accurate. In *Henry V,* Shakespeare changed several of the small historical facts, and changed dates and times to make them fit the story better. But, although most of his version of Agincourt is accurate, there is at least one big error: the English fought mostly with the longbow while Shakespeare's play mostly shows hand-to-hand combat between nobles. In the 1500s, just like today, people wanted heroes and, because it was more dramatic to have the leaders fighting each other, Shakespeare gave the nobles more important roles than they probably had in the actual battle.

(422 words)

Language note

Plays are divided into acts, scenes and lines. The St. Crispian speech is in the fourth act, third scene and lines 57–67. This is written as: 4.3.57–67 or IV.iii. 57–67

Into Battle!

Vocabulary notes

1. **band** (noun) a group of people who work together to achieve the same aims
2. **defeat** (verb) to win a victory over someone in a war, competition, game, etc.
3. **shall** (modal verb) used to say what will happen or must happen
4. **vile** (adjective) very unpleasant

Read and listen again to practice your pronunciation.

Concepts

Shakespeare added several thousand words and phrases to the English language, some of which are still common, such as *manhood* (qualities such as strength and courage that people think a man should have) and *shed blood* (to kill or injure people, especially during a war or a fight). Others, although not common, are easy to guess such as *accursed* (someone who has had a curse put on them) and *now-a-bed* (sleeping). Some, however, are more difficult to understand such as *gentle his condition* (change his manner).

After you read

A. Summarize the main idea in one sentence.

French records of King Henry's famous speech say that he simply told his soldiers that he and the other nobles weren't worried if the French won because they would simply be captured and ransomed. The common soldier, however, was worth little and so they had better fight hard or they could be killed.

Culture note

Many lines from Shakespeare have been used for the titles of books and movies. In this scene, "band of brothers" was used for a mini-series based on American army experiences in World War II.

B. Vocabulary check: Use the clues to fill in the crossword.

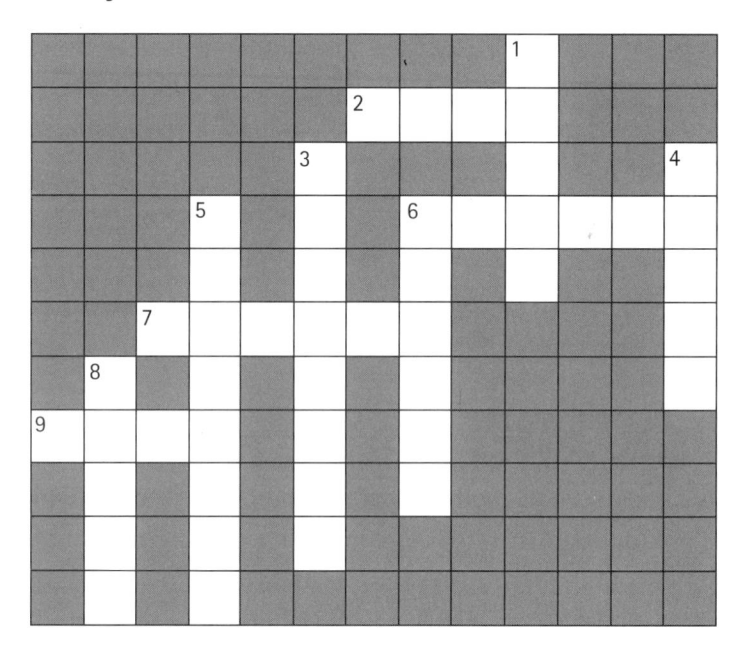

Down
1. to alter to suit needs
3. a captured soldier
4. something to protect you in battle
5. to search through unwanted things
6. fighting
8. His speech helped _____ the troops.

Across
2. a group of people
6. the person who captures someone
7. a fee paid for the return of someone
9. an antonym of *clothed*

> **Language note**
>
> An *oxymoron* is a pair of words that go together but mean opposite things, like a *fine mess* or *friendly fight*. People humorously say that *military intelligence* is an oxymoron.

Into Battle!

C. Choose the best answer.

1. The general __a__ the troops to fight hard.
   a. fired
   b. rallied
   c. adapted
   d. exhausted

2. Which statement is not true? The English won the Battle of Agincourt because they __d__.
   a. were very patient
   b. enticed the enemy to charge
   c. could move about more easily
   d. were fighting on their own land

3. *The English were outnumbered three to one* means there were __c__.
   a. fewer English than French
   b. more English than French
   c. three times as many French as English
   d. half as many French as English

4. A synonym for *exhausted* is __d__.
   a. English
   b. victorious
   c. smoke
   d. tired

5. The phrase *Gentle his condition* means __b__.
   a. improve his health
   b. make him a better person
   c. better the weather forecast
   d. calm his nerves

6. *The battle was mostly won by mud* means that __c__.
   a. mud exhausted the English army
   b. mud helped the English be more mobile
   c. the muddy conditions gave the English an advantage
   d. the English used mud as a weapon

7. Charles VI was __c__.
   a. a great playwright
   b. a great soldier
   c. the King of England
   d. the King of France

8. *Hold their manhoods cheap* means __c__.
   a. be confident
   b. be ashamed
   c. be proud
   d. be tired

9. The phrase *from this day to the ending of the world* means __b__.
   a. until now
   b. quite often
   c. time immemorial
   d. from this day forward

10. The Old English contraction *ne'er* means __d__.
    a. nor
    b. every
    c. neither
    d. never

Exam strategy

Always make sure you read the instructions carefully. Often, students overlook instructions such as *answer one of the three questions* or *answer all three*.

Debate

Take one side, add your own ideas and debate in pairs or groups.

For: There are always many sides to history.	*Against:* History is just a tool to teach us about the past.
Points:	*Points:*
• The French have a different story of Agincourt.	• Shakespeare's version tells us the heart of the truth.
• The French say the English did not fight fair.	• The lessons from Agincourt are that a small group with intelligence can defeat a great foe.
• Henry killed the prisoners for no good reason.	• Some parts of the battle may have been an accident.
• _people always has different side_	• _____
• _history can be change_	• _____
• _different contry has different opion_	• _____

Debate strategy

When you debate, always try to speak as if you are confident and know what you are talking about. Don't sound like you doubt what you are saying or may have thought something else before. Don't use expressions such as, *I think* or *I feel*.

Say:
- "This is the truth. The ... ."
- "It has always been the case that ... ."
- "There is absolutely no question that ... ."

Another idea to debate

A popular saying is that *history is always written by the victor.* This means that the winner's version of events is usually taken to be the truth. Do you agree?

Learn more

Read about another battle. Find examples of strategy and report them to your class.

> Would you like to buy some second hand armor and a horse?

Look online

Check out the website at www.read-and-think.com for extra learning resources.

Add new words to your personal dictionary on page 146.

UNIT 10
**Education
Computing**

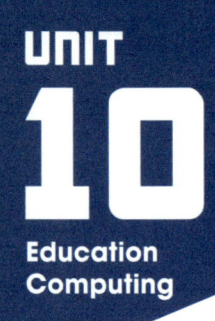

The Future of Education
Lesson One

Before you read

- How long have universities been around?
- What is the future of universities?

What's happening in the pictures?

Aspects of student life

Read about it

- What image do many people have of what a university should look like?
- What is special about Oxford University?

An Ancient and Modern University

Many people have a classical image of what they think a university should look like. This image is usually something to do with old stone buildings covered in ivy. Many modern universities around the world are still built in this classic style in order to imitate the early style of England's first universities, including Oxford and Cambridge universities.

Ivy-covered walls at Oxford University

Oxford University is the oldest English-speaking university in the world. Professors there have taught students for centuries, beginning around 1096. The university swiftly expanded for political reasons. In 1167, England's King Henry II (1133–1189) banned English students from attending the University of Paris so students who had planned to go there now had to go to a university in England. But even though students were discouraged from traveling to study in Paris, Oxford soon began inviting international students. International students often introduce new ideas when they attend a university so the benefits go both ways.

In its long history, Oxford has had many controversies and accomplishments. For example, in the thirteenth century, there were riots between what was called "town and gown" (townspeople and students who dressed in academic gowns). Because of these conflicts, residence halls were established so students would not need to live in the town. These residences were replaced by the first of Oxford's colleges, each under the supervision of a master who was responsible for the students who stayed there.

Merton College, Oxford

During most of Oxford's history, women were not welcome. The university was mostly for training men who would enter the church. It was not until 1878 that academic halls were established for women. And women waited until 1920 to become full members of the university. Since 1974, all of Oxford's thirty-nine colleges admit both men and women except one: St. Hilda's, a women's college.

(297 words)

Stone gargoyle, Oxford

Reading strategy

An important reading strategy is *predicting*, thinking about what might happen in a passage or just what an author will say next in an argument or story. Predicting helps build reading comprehension.

Vocabulary notes

1. **admit** (verb) to let someone or something enter a place or join a club or organization
2. **ban** (verb) to officially say that something must not be done, used, etc.
3. **century** (noun) a period of 100 years, used especially in giving dates
4. **classical** (adjective) based on a traditional set of ideas
5. **college** (noun) a place where students study after they leave school
6. **controversy** (noun) a serious disagreement and argument among many people about something over a long period of time
7. **ivy** (noun) a climbing plant with dark green shiny leaves
8. **swiftly** (adverb) happening or moving very quickly and smoothly

Add new words to your personal dictionary on page 146.

Read and listen again to practice your pronunciation.

After you read

A. Answer these questions.

1. What "first" is Oxford famous for?
2. Who was not allowed to attend Oxford for most of its history?
3. Why might the term "town and gown" be popular?
4. How did a king help Oxford become more popular?
5. Why might a university invite international students?

Understand what you read

Contractions

A contraction is the shortening of two words and putting them together. The missing part is replaced with an apostrophe ('). Contractions are very common in spoken English and informal written English, but not all are used in written English. The most common contractions are based on the words *am, is, are, has, have, had, will* and *would*. They are used in contractions with certain nouns (*John's at the park.*), pronouns (*I'll go, too.*) and question words (*Who's in the car?*).

Here are four tips for working with contractions:
- Only use contractions in informal writing. For formal writing, write out the full words.
- If you're not sure whether the text is formal or informal, use the full form.
- There are many contractions in spoken English that are never written out. For example, *The books're on the shelf.* would be written as *The books are on the shelf.*

Computer note

Most word processors will automatically correct a word such as (*theyve*) adding the apostrophe (*they've*) in the right place. But don't be lazy; check your work.

Language note

A *virtual university* is one that mostly (or only) offers its courses on the Internet.

B. Rewrite the sentences, writing out the contractions.

1. A university must serve the public; it shouldn't just be for the rich.
   _____

2. He's an expert and knows more about ants than anyone in the world.
   _____

3. You'll need two things for university: an interest in learning and time to study.
   _____

4. I would've gone to university, if I'd done better in school.
   _____

5. There's only one rule to education: think.
   _____

C. Fill in the missing words. Use the correct form of the word.

- **bachelor's degree** (noun) a first university degree
- **degree** (noun) a course at a university, or the qualification given to someone who has successfully finished the course
- **doctorate** (noun) a university degree at the highest level
- **institution** (noun) a large important organization such as a university, church, or bank
- **master's degree** (noun) a university degree that you can get by studying for one or two years after your first degree

A university is an ___institution___ of higher learning where students receive an education and are granted ___degree___ based upon their individual course of studies. A university will usually grant ___doctorate___ and in many instances will also offer ___bachelor's degree___ and ___master's degree___ degree programs.

What other ways can you define a university? Think about what else a university does.

What about you?

What is a new and exciting course you would like to take at university? Write a title and a short description. Remember to think of an assignment the students would have to do to show they understood the course.

Lesson Two

Read about it

- What was once the main purpose of educating men?
- What part did Asian governments have in educating their citizens?

The Growth of Asian Universities

Greek and Roman ideas about education influenced Western universities a great deal. Even the word *university* comes from the Latin word *universitas*. Similarly, *college* is taken from *collegium*. Another common Latin word is *corpus*, which refers to a body of work but is also the root of the word *corporation*, a large business.

Asia's educational roots are different from and began far earlier than those of Europe. In China, formal education was popular at least as early as the Shang Dynasty (1766–1050 BC). At this time, however, education was not for everyone. Instead, only the wealthiest and most important people attended school.

The main purpose of China's education system at this time was to turn out government officials.

Students hard at work at Nanking University, China, early 1900s.

Reading strategy

If you need to form an inference about what you read, look for things that are hinted at but not directly said.

The first curriculum focused on religious rites (to please the gods), music, archery, chariot racing, history and mathematics. However, the curriculum changed with the teachings of Confucius (551–479 BC). During the Spring and Autumn, and Warring States period (770–221 BC), the physical side of education was dropped and people began studying the ideals of society, government and personal behavior. It was this idea of education that spread throughout Asia. After it was introduced to Korea, Japan and other Asian nations, it was adapted by them to suit their own needs and ideas.

Until recently, however, most governments in Asia did not take part in actively educating their citizens. Instead, they followed China's model of civil service examinations using essay questions. The best writers were selected to be government officials. Students who wanted to prepare for these examinations enrolled in private schools. Modern universities that were open to all eventually followed, as Asian students traveled to other countries and saw how those university systems worked. As these students became more aware of Western ideas, they shared them, adopting the ones that were most suitable to their own situations.

(312 words)

University students today still work hard, but have a more relaxed lifestyle

Vocabulary notes

1. **curriculum** (noun) all of the subjects that are taught at a school, college, etc.
2. **enroll** (verb) to become or make someone officially a member of a course, school, etc.
3. **ideal** (noun) a principle or belief that seems good
4. **influence** (verb) to have an effect on the way someone or something develops, behaves or thinks
5. **rites** (noun) a traditional ceremony that is always performed in the same way, especially for a religious purpose
6. **roots** (noun) the origins of something
7. **turn out** (verb) to produce or make something

Read and listen again to practice your pronunciation.

After you read

A. Summarize the main idea in one sentence.

How much school is enough? Most people go to school until they are young adults and some go on to university. A degree was more than enough for anyone a few years ago, but now people believe in the idea of lifelong learning. Lifelong learning suggests that people should never stop picking up new ideas and skills.

_____

B. Vocabulary check: Fill in the missing letters to find the secret word.

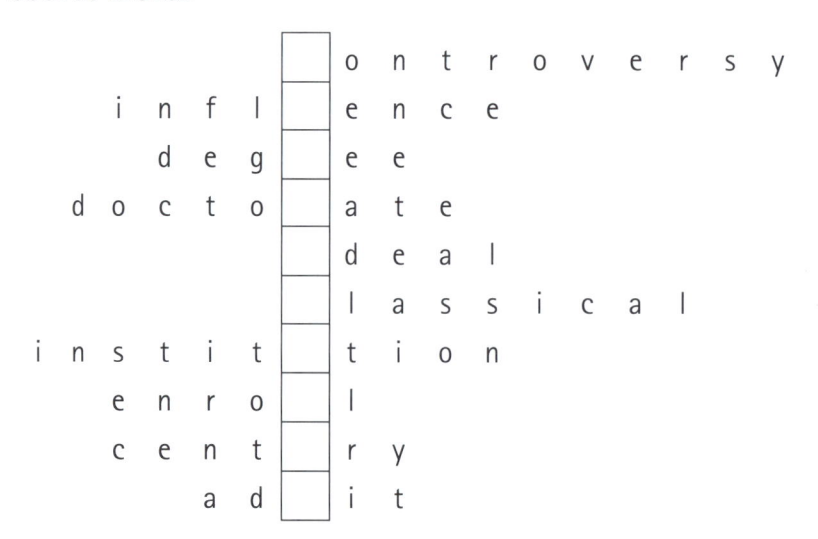

```
           c o n t r o v e r s y
    i n f l u e n c e
      d e g r e e
  d o c t o r a t e
          i d e a l
          c l a s s i c a l
i n s t i t u t i o n
    e n r o l
    c e n t r y
        a d m i t
```

Culture note

The Classics is a term used to refer to essential reading, usually important older or ancient writings. Different cultures have different classics. What are yours?

C. Choose the best answer.

1. ___ is the oldest English-speaking university in the world.
   a. Oxford University
   b. Cambridge University
   c. University of Paris
   d. St. Hilda's College

2. Residence halls were established because ___ .
   a. there was an effort to copy the architecture of England
   b. women became full members of the university
   c. English students were banned from going abroad to study
   d. there was too much fighting between students and townspeople

3. Residence halls were replaced by ___ .
   a. academic halls
   b. colleges
   c. buildings
   d. universities

4. Many new universities are built ___ .
   a. without residences and academic halls
   b. in the style of the eleventh century
   c. to look like foreign universities in England
   d. of plastic with plants growing up the front

5. A synonym for *riots* is ___ .
   a. explanations
   b. fighting
   c. agreements
   d. accomplishments

6. Banning English students from attending other universities but inviting international students might be described as a ___ .
   a. controversy
   b. compliment
   c. contradiction
   d. accomplishment

7. Education was for the wealthy and important because ___ .
   a. the unimportant were not smart enough
   b. the poor were mostly government officials
   c. the poor could not afford university
   d. the unimportant did not have the right sort of personality

8. A synonym for *roots* might be ___ .
   a. scope
   b. growth
   c. origins
   d. branches

> **Exam strategy**
>
> In essay questions, make sure your writing is easy to read. Don't rush so much that your letters turn into something that the teacher can't understand.

Debate

Take one side, add your own ideas and debate in pairs or groups.

For: Universities continue to adapt to the needs of society.	*Against:* Universities are no longer relevant and will soon disappear.
Points:	*Points:*
• People will always need to have basic training for whatever they do.	• People can now learn virtually, on the WWW.
• You can't "learn on the job" in medicine and other fields.	• Universities can't keep up with the skills people need for today's jobs.
• Universities preserve and share the learning of centuries past.	• Most people forget most of what they have learned by the time they graduate.
• _____	• _____
• _____	• _____
• _____	• _____

Debate strategy

When you debate, don't bring your personal views and experiences into the argument. It's better to stick to the key points of your arguments.

Don't say:

- "Once when I was twelve years old, I had a similar problem … ."

Say:

- "Something that has happened to every twelve-year-old is … ."

More ideas to debate

"Learning makes the wise wiser and the fool more foolish."
John Ray (1627-1705) English naturalist

"Education is what remains when we have forgotten all that we have been taught."
George Savile (1633-1695) English politician, author

"I have never let my schooling interfere with my education."
Mark Twain (1835-1910) American writer

"The principal goal of education is to create men who are capable of doing new things, not simply of repeating what other generations have done."
Jean Piaget (1896-1980) Swiss psychologist

Learn more

What makes a university good? Look on the WWW at several websites for famous universities and see what things they think are important enough to put on their homepage. Report your examples to your class.

Look online

Check out the website at www.read-and-think.com for extra learning resources.

> **Language note**
>
> In older writing, the words *he*, *men* and *mankind* are often used to refer to people in general. Today this is considered poor style.

Add new words to your personal dictionary on page 146.

UNIT 11

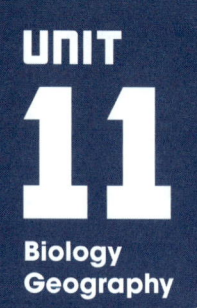

**Biology
Geography**

Extinct!
Lesson One

Before you read

- How do species become extinct?
- Why do extinctions affect us?

What is happening in the pictures?

Extinct!

Read about it

- How are the ideas connected?
- What do islands have to do with extinction?

Island Biogeography

One of the questions that has puzzled scientists for many years is how to predict the rate of extinction among species of animals, birds, insects and plants in different parts of the world. In 1967, Robert MacArthur and Edward Wilson proposed a theory that tried to answer this. To make it easier to measure and explain, they based their theory on islands.

Rarotonga, Cook Islands

In fact, MacArthur and Wilson's islands are not just considered as islands in an ocean surrounded by water, but also islands of nature surrounded by cities, factories or farms. MacArthur and Wilson's concern was how the number of species found on an island is balanced between migration and extinction. They explained that the number of species on an island depends on:

- the size of the island,
- the shape of the island (especially the height of its hills and mountains),
- how close the island is to a source of new species,
- how rich in species the source area is, and
- the balance between rates of migration of new species and extinction of existing species.

Reading strategy

If you need to read to consider an argument, look for the main points and the evidence in the passage. This can make more efficient your reading by not wasting time looking at other points.

MacArthur and Wilson's theory showed that if these islands are not protected, the species on them will disappear, some of them forever. Moreover, the theory helped to predict how the loss of one species of animal, bird, insect or plant could affect other species and lead to their loss as well.

Because of the theory, many fragile habitats around the world have been protected from development. Many of these habitats are in the form of nature reserves. However, there have been many criticisms of the theory, and many scientists think it is too difficult to measure how an island's ecology works. They have also suggested that even when an island is isolated, creatures still find their way there. Cities, for example, are often thought of as the opposite of wilderness, but countless animals, birds, insects and plants live with people, including many wild animals.

(324 words)

Yellowbilled hornhill catches a locust

Vocabulary notes

1. **development** (noun) the process of becoming bigger, better, more important, etc., or the result of this process
2. **ecology** (noun) the way in which plants, animals, and people are related to each other and to their environment, or the study of this
3. **extinction** (noun) when a type of animal or plant no longer exists
4. **habitat** (noun) the natural environment in which a plant or animal lives
5. **propose** (verb) to officially suggest a plan
6. **species** (noun) a group of animals or plants of the same kind
7. **theory** (noun) an explanation for something that has not yet been proved to be true

Language note

The prefix *eco-* comes from the Greek word meaning *house*. It's most commonly used in the word *ecology*, which means the study of an environment. But *eco-* is now used on many new words such as *ecotourism*.

Add new words to your personal dictionary on page 146.

Read and listen again to practice your pronunciation.

After you read

A. Answer these questions.

1. Why did MacArthur and Wilson propose their theory?
2. What do they mean by "islands"?
3. What has been a benefit of the theory?
4. What happens if an island is not protected?
5. *Bio-* means *life*. What does *biogeography* mean?

Understand what you read

Prepositions

Prepositions show relationships between other words in a sentence. Often, they help explain where something is in time and space.

Time

Use *at* with specific times: *The plane lands at 2:15 p.m.* For specific dates, use *on*: *It's on Monday, May 6.* Use *in* when you are talking about something that happened during a day, month, season or year: *I like to hike in summer.*

Space

Use *on* with surfaces (*on a desk*), small islands (*on the Isle of Man*) and directions (*on the left*). Use *in* with spaces (*in a city or park*), bodies of water (*in a stream or lake*) and lines (*stand in a line*). Use *at* with places (*at the fountain*), places on a page (*at the bottom of the page*), groups of people (*at the rear of the crowd*).

Here are four tips for working with prepositions:
- There are many exceptions to the rules that must be memorized.
- Prepositions may not seem logical: we lie *in* a bed, but *on* a couch.
- Some prepositions are different depending on where exactly you are: Should we meet *at* the theater or *in* the theater?
- In English, it's OK to end a sentence with a preposition: *What are you looking at?*

Culture note

In 1762, Bishop Robert Lowth (1710–1787), published a guide to grammar, including the rule that you can't end a sentence with a preposition. But the rule was based on Latin, not English. Winston Churchill (1874–1965) showed how silly the rule was with the sentence, "That is nonsense up with which I shall not put."

B. Fill in the prepositions.

1. He was born ___in___ 1957 ___on___ April 1st.
2. My test is ___on___ Monday ___at___ another school.
3. We'll meet ___at___ Stanley Park ___on___ six o'clock.
4. He won the top spelling prize ___at___ our country ___in___ 2004.
5. ___In___ winter, we ski ___at___ a Korean resort.

C. Fill in the missing words. Use the correct form of the word.

- **accumulate** (verb) to gradually increase in quantity until there is a large quantity in one place
- **cancer** (noun) a serious disease in which cells in someone's body grow in a way that is not normal
- **contaminate** (verb) to make something dirty or dangerous by adding something such as chemicals or poison to it
- **food chain** (noun) animals and plants considered as a group, in which one animal is eaten by another animal, which is eaten by another, etc.
- **pesticide** (noun) a chemical substance used to kill insects that damage crops

Silent Spring is a book by Rachel Carson that describes how a ___food chain___, DDT, enters the ___accumulate___ and ___contaminate___ in plants, insects and animals, including human beings, causing ___cancer___ and death. Carson found that DDT and other pesticides had ___pesticide___ the entire world food supply. DDT was eventually banned in the United States, but it is still produced there and sold in other countries.

In what other ways do we damage the environment?

What about you?

Different plants, insects and animals help us in different ways. Other than humans, what do you think would be the most important animal to save from extinction? Why?

Choose me!

Choose me!

124

Lesson Two

Read about it

- How does this article differ from the point of view of the article in Lesson One?
- What is fact and what is opinion?

Reading strategy

An important reading strategy is connecting what you are reading to what you already know. Take time to find connections and think about what is similar and what is different to what you know.

How Many Species Become Extinct Each Year?

Pandas, native to China, have become the symbol of animals threatened with extinction

Since MacArthur and Wilson published their theory about how island species become extinct, people have become used to "facts" such as the extinction of as many as 100,000 species per year. People worry that we are using up the world's natural resources and the Earth will no longer be able to support all the people on it. A popular advertisement talks about the plants in the Amazon region. It says these plants may contain a new cure for a disease, and they may be lost if the area is not protected. But exactly how many species die each year? Do we believe "facts" about high numbers because they seem like they are correct or because we have actually measured them?

Giant tortoises have been extinct on Mauritius for 200 years; today, the species is being reintroduced from nearby islands

Predictions of animal, bird, insect and plant extinctions are based on the idea that when one plant or animal disappears, many others follow. If, for example, a plant is lost because we build a city or a road where there was once a jungle, the insect that lives on the plant also dies. Then the bird that eats the insect dies and so on. All in all, the world is becoming a worse place as we destroy our natural resources.

Economist Julian L. Simon (1932–1998), disagreed. "Our species is better off in just about every ... way," he said. "Just about every important long-term measure of human material welfare shows improvement over the decades and centuries, in the United States and the rest of the world. Raw materials—all of them—have become less scarce rather than more. The air in the U.S. and in other rich countries is safer to breathe. Water cleanliness has improved. The environment is increasingly healthy, with every prospect that this trend will continue.

Cheetahs are close to extinction in their native Africa and the Middle East

"Fear is rampant about rapid rates of species extinction," he said, "but the fear has little or no basis. The highest rate of observed extinction, though certainly more have gone extinct unobserved, is *one* species per year ... ." The higher estimates did not come from observation, they came from theory.

(345 words)

Vocabulary notes

1. **estimate** (noun) what you think the value, size, etc., of something is, after calculating it quickly
2. **observation** (noun) the process of watching someone or something carefully
3. **resource** (noun) something that a country, organization, person, etc., has which they can use
4. **scarce** (adjective) if food, clothing, water, etc., is scarce, there is not enough of it available

Read and listen again to practice your pronunciation.

Extinct!

After you read

A. Summarize the main idea in one sentence.

In the 1900s, the forests of Puerto Rico were reduced by ninety-nine percent and most of the species on the island became extinct. However, by the 1980s, most of the forest had grown back and ninety-seven species of birds were present, compared to only sixty species living there before 1492.

196 Puerto Rico was a extited in island and 97 species of brid in 1980

B. Vocabulary check: Find the words.

R	D	W	R	A	U	S	I	E	S	J	I	R	F	V
L	E	A	X	E	Z	R	M	X	C	D	L	A	H	O
H	V	U	P	O	S	E	M	T	A	A	H	K	A	N
O	E	C	R	F	P	D	N	I	R	A	S	A	B	T
B	L	A	O	E	E	M	F	N	C	C	R	N	I	A
S	O	N	P	D	C	X	R	C	E	R	B	I	T	M
E	P	C	O	R	I	Q	A	T	T	P	S	I	A	I
R	M	E	S	C	E	E	F	I	S	E	O	H	T	N
V	E	R	E	C	S	C	I	O	P	S	S	P	S	A
A	N	D	C	Q	R	O	M	N	E	T	N	E	T	T
T	T	V	I	B	I	L	N	S	P	I	C	K	E	N
I	V	N	T	H	E	O	R	Y	I	C	M	I	E	D
O	N	J	G	R	L	G	U	G	E	I	C	C	O	E
N	E	W	H	Y	S	Y	E	V	S	D	E	N	R	G
R	E	S	O	U	R	C	E	S	C	E	M	A	Y	I

cancer	extinction	pesticide	scarce
development	habitat	propose	species
ecology	observation	resource	theory

Language note

What do you add when an abbreviation ends a sentence? Nothing. There is no need to add a second period if the abbreviation already has one.

127

C. Choose the best answer.

1. The number of species found on an island is balanced between __c__.
   a. the new species arriving and other species dying out
   b. the course of the new and old species
   c. the size and shape of the island
   d. the number, location and speed of the species

2. The number of species on an island does not depend on __a__.
   a. the variety of wildlife
   b. the geography of the island
   c. the movement of animals
   d. the nature of the ocean

3. The purpose of a nature reserve is to __c__
   a. measure the environment for scientific study
   b. maintain the landscape against new species that might destroy it
   c. protect environments from being built on
   d. surround cities, factories and farms with nature

4. *Human material welfare* refers to __b__
   a. the health of people
   b. ways to measure that people are better off
   c. the opposite of warfare
   d. the possessions of people

5. *Biogeography* refers to the study of ___. __a__
   a. living things and their environment
   b. nature's species and rocks and minerals
   c. maps of nature
   d. the protection of land masses

6. Critics of the theory believe ___. __a__
   a. it's impossible to stop development
   b. immigration and extinction are inevitable
   c. island ecology is too complex to reduce it to a simple theory
   d. islands don't need protection from development

7. The author highlights "facts" with quotation marks ___. __b__
   a. to highlight the truth of this fact
   b. to use the word fact in a special way
   c. to question the truth of this statement
   d. instead of using italics

8. *Fragile habitats* refers to __a__.
   a. sensitive environments
   b. breakable areas
   c. gentle habits
   d. frequent kindness

Exam strategy

When preparing for an exam, it helps to study in the same atmosphere as the place you'll take the test. Study with good light at a desk or table with the music and TV turned off.

Extinct!

Debate

Take one side, add your own ideas and debate in pairs or groups.

For: People are destroying the world's environment.	*Against:* The environment is quite tough and will survive.
Points:	*Points:*
• Soon there will only be rats and cockroaches left.	• The example of Puerto Rico shows that nature heals itself.
• Governments protect their own interests, such as collecting taxes from large companies, rather than preserving the environment.	• People like bad news, but science solves many of our problems.
• People think of short-term personal gain rather than what is good for the world.	• The world is much larger than most people think.
• they're huge extincted number of money	• animal
• human cares more than animals	•
• trees are cutting down everyday	•

Debate strategy

When you debate, never say that you agree with your opponent or suggest there's a compromise between your two points. Make sure you are clearly supporting your points and attacking your opponents' throughout the debate.

Don't say:
- "I guess I never thought about that."
- "I suppose you have a good point there."
- "Maybe if we took part of what I say and part of what you say, we could ... ."

Say:
- "This is no time for half-measures or compromises. We must all agree with my point that ... ."

Another idea to debate

"Here in the U.S. we turn our rivers and streams into sewers and dumping grounds, we pollute the air, we destroy our forests and exterminate fishes, birds and mammals—not to speak of vulgarizing charming landscapes with hideous advertisements."
Theodore Roosevelt (1858–1919), U.S. President writing in 1915

Learn more

Use the library or the WWW to find an example of a plant, animal or insect that has become extinct. Report what you find to your class.

Look online

Check out the website at www.read-and-think.com for extra learning resources.

> Add new words to your personal dictionary on page 146.

Angels or Outcasts?

Lesson One

Before you read

- In what ways can you permanently change your appearance?
- What kinds of changes are OK? What kinds of changes aren't OK?

What's different about these people?

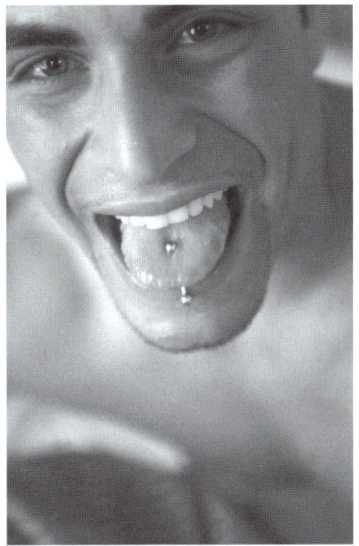

Tattoos and piercing are becoming increasingly popular

UNIT 12
Psychology
Sociology
Medicine

Culture note

Are you ethnocentric or culturally sensitive? *Ethnocentric* is the term for people who look at other cultures and practices and think that the other cultures are "wrong" simply because they are different from their own. *Culturally sensitive* is the term for people who aren't ethnocentric; such people are open to understanding other cultures.

Read about it

- What does the title mean?
- What does the title tell you about the writer's attitude?

I Love Your Wings!

Dr. Joe Rosen is a well-known American plastic surgeon, and he thinks you should be able to change your appearance, any way you like. He thinks you should have wings if you want. He'd also like you to have a tail and extra thumbs or fingers, too.

The idea of extra body parts is not so odd. People already modify their bodies in many ways, such as piercing their ears for earrings. Metal pieces are often added to other body parts: the nose, lips, belly button and even the tongue. People who lose a body part in an accident are sometimes given a new one, either from another person or something man-made.

Fifty years ago, plastic surgery—to improve your appearance rather than for medical reasons—was uncommon, but now people increasingly use surgery to look younger and better. Sometimes this involves making a nose smaller or getting rid of wrinkles. Why not also add something useful? Dr. Rosen once met a waiter who was born with an extra thumb on one hand. The extra thumb made the waiter excellent at his work by letting him carry plates more easily. Perhaps other people would like to have an extra thumb for other jobs. There might even be new jobs that could be done by people with extra fingers. For example, what new

Reading strategy

Skim the passage looking for key words that are new to you. If they seem important to understanding the passage and aren't easy to understand in context, look them up before you start to read.

music could a pianist play with seven or nine fingers on each hand?

Dr. Rosen could probably give you wings but they would not help you fly; the human body and its bones are too heavy. To fly, we would probably need to replace our bones with hollow ones, like birds have. But at least you would be able to flutter your wings, thanks to a wonder of the brain called *body mapping* that controls new limbs.

Many people have plastic surgery to feel better about themselves. Perhaps new wings would make you feel like an angel.

(320 words)

Vocabulary notes

1. **belly button** (noun) the small hole just below your waist on the front of your body
2. **modify** (verb) to make small changes to something in order to improve it
3. **plastic surgery** (noun) medical treatment to improve the way someone's face or body looks
4. **wrinkle** (noun) a small line on the skin on your face that you get when you are old

Add new words to your personal dictionary on page 146.

Read and listen again to practice your pronunciation.

After you read

A. Answer these questions.

1. Why would a person with wings not be able to fly?
2. What is Dr. Rosen's job?
3. Why might some people want extra fingers?
4. What are different reasons for plastic surgery?
5. Why do many people have plastic surgery?

Understand what you read

Colons, em-dashes and semicolons

Writers often separate one or more parts of a sentence with punctuation. Different ways of doing this have different purposes.

:	—	;
colon	em-dash	semicolon

A *colon* is often followed by a series of ideas or examples, set off by commas or semicolons.

- *Scarring is done in several ways: branding with hot metal; cutting the skin; and cutting the skin and rubbing in ash.*

Pairs of *em-dashes* are often used to show a clarification or contrasting information in the middle of a sentence.

- *Around the world—not just in Africa—people have used scarring to change their appearance.*

A *semicolon* is often used to show a related thought, even though the thought could stand as a separate sentence.

- *Traditional societies have also used simple surgery to change their appearance; the warriors of one African tribe cut off one of their ears.*

Computer note

Colons and semicolons are easy to mistype when you work at the computer; be sure to check your writing.

B. Add colons, em-dashes or semicolons.

1. Plastic surgery just for beauty has a different name cosmetic surgery.
2. Reasons for plastic surgery not just for medical needs are quickly changing.
3. Plastic surgery now has many uses improving looks losing weight correcting physical problems.
4. No one knows what problems an operation may bring be careful.
5. There are good reasons for changing the way we look to feel better to look younger to lose dangerous weight.

C. Fill in the missing words. Use the correct form the word.

- **complication** (noun) a problem that makes a situation more difficult to understand or deal with
- **diverse** (adjective) very different from each other
- **evaluate** (verb) to carefully consider something or someone in order to decide how good or bad they are
- **extensive** (adjective) large in amount or area
- **facility** (noun) a service or feature that a machine or system has
- **qualification** (noun) a skill or quality that you need to do a job

Many people travel to have _____ kinds of plastic surgery. Such a trip can include a vacation and a less expensive operation. However, there can be many _____ . First, you may not be able to _____ the _____ of the staff; they may not even be doctors. Second, the medical _____ may not be safe. And third, you may need _____ follow-up care—which can be expensive back home—after your surgery. All in all, one should think cautiously about combining pleasure and surgery.

What about you?

Lots of people wear tattoos, but some people only wear them for a short time—they are temporary tattoos. Design your own temporary tattoo in the box.

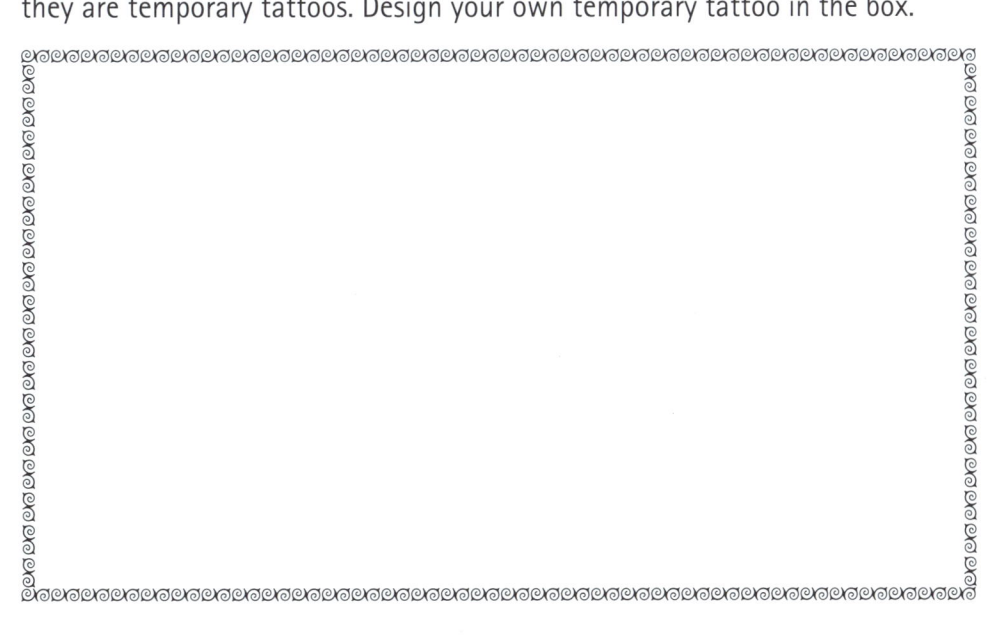

Lesson Two

Read about it

- What is an outcast?
- What does the title tell you about the writer's attitude?

Making Outcasts

Most people think that plastic surgery is quite new, but it's not. As far back as three thousand years ago, the ancient Egyptians practiced a simple form of plastic surgery, taking skin from one part of the body to repair wounds and burns on another part. Of course, these operations were done for medical reasons, not just because people wanted to look different. Now plastic surgery has become more common and operations to change the shape of one's eyes or nose or even removing the lower ribs to make one's waist smaller are quite common.

But sadly, plastic surgeons have gone past these ideas; healing or creating beauty is no longer enough. Many people want to be ugly or, at the very least, less human. In particular, people have had many other kinds of operations for the purpose of modifying their faces and bodies to make them more animal-like. One man has had horns inserted into his skull. Many

Body art: the question is no longer *What is possible?*

Reading strategy

To help your reading comprehension, make notes in pencil in your books (but not in library books!). When you read a second time, erase notes you understand and underline notes that are more important.

so-called "lizard people" have had their tongues split and scales tattooed onto their skin. One woman has had multiple operations to make her look like a cat. She has had hair inserted into her face to make her look like she has cat whiskers. Some have added long artificial teeth to make them look more like dogs. Other people have gone beyond different kinds of tattoos to getting their entire bodies covered with what look like fish scales or even fur.

The question that needs to be asked is not, *What is possible?* The important question is, *What is wrong with such outcasts?* There are two answers: they lack self-respect and they have a desperate need for attention. They should be treated by psychiatrists, not plastic surgeons. There are limits to the benefits of plastic surgery. We already have a society that doesn't want to look old. We should beware of a society that no longer wants to look human.

(318 words)

> **Reading strategy**
>
> An important reading strategy is reflecting. Take time to sit back and think about what you have read and how it fits with what you know and how you feel. This is especially important for passages based on opinions.

Vocabulary notes

1. **desperate** (adjective) willing to do anything to change a bad situation, even if it is dangerous or unpleasant
2. **horn** (noun) one of the two hard pointed parts that grows on the heads of cows, goats, etc., or the substance this is made of
3. **outcast** (noun) someone who is not accepted by other people
4. **psychiatrist** (noun) a doctor who treats people who have a mental illness
5. **rib** (noun) one of the pairs of curved bones in your chest
6. **waist** (noun) the part around the middle of your body just above your hips

Read and listen again to practice your pronunciation.

After you read

Language note

Numbers and dates at the start of a sentence are usually written out. In this paragraph, *Today* can also refer to current times, not the actual day.

A. Summarize the main idea in one sentence.

Seven thousand years ago, the Ainu of Japan tattooed themselves for religious reasons. As early as 297 AD, Japanese men tattooed their faces and bodies. But by the seventh century, Japanese rulers used tattooing to identify and punish criminals. Around 1700, only royals could wear beautiful clothing; other Japanese men used full-body tattoos to get around the rule. Today, tattooed human skins are kept in special museums.

_____

B. Vocabulary check: Use the clues to fill in the crossword.

Down
1. change
2. a bone in your chest
4. a doctor of the mind
5. someone who doesn't belong to any group of people

Across
3. unexpected problem
6. a place such as a hospital
7. A test is one way to ___ you.
8. an antonym for *the same*

138

C. Choose the best answer.

1. Plastic surgery ___ .
   a. was first used to help people with wounds and burns
   b. was invented to make people look like animals
   c. uses various kinds of plastic, such as shopping bags
   d. can be done by anyone at home in the kitchen

2. Some people may get plastic surgery to ___ .
   a. pierce their teeth
   b. make themselves unhappy
   c. make themselves look more like animals
   d. increase their weight

3. The author of *I Love Your Wings!* probably feels ___ .
   a. everyone should have wings
   b. a tail could be useful in many situations
   c. most waiters should have several thumbs
   d. there are few limits on how we might change our looks

4. The author of *Making Outcasts* probably feels ___ .
   a. most plastic surgery makes you look better
   b. laws should govern the practice of plastic surgery
   c. no one wants to look like a cat
   d. many new kinds of plastic surgery are possible

5. The fact that plastic surgery wasn't common fifty years ago suggests ___ .
   a. ideas about what is acceptable are changing
   b. there are now techniques to make horns popular
   c. people preferred plastic surgery
   d. it is best done by doctors

6. In *I Love Your Wings!*, the phrase *body mapping* refers to ___ .
   a. a kind of tattooing
   b. making maps with bodies
   c. the mind's way of recognizing new limbs
   d. body tattoos of maps

7. In *Making Outcasts* the phrase *treated by psychiatrists, not plastic surgeons* suggests ___ .
   a. people have many choices of doctors
   b. people may have problems with their minds, not their looks
   c. psychiatrists offer people more treats
   d. people may not know about their choice of doctors

8. A general idea in the two passages is ___ .
   a. plastic surgery is good
   b. we will all soon wear wings
   c. plastic surgery is bad
   d. people have good and bad reasons for changing their looks

> **Exam strategy**
>
> Measure the time you spend on each question according to the marks. If a question is worth 50%, spend 50% of your time on it. If it's only worth 10%, spend much less time.

Face to face Debate

Take one side, add your own ideas and debate in pairs or groups.

For: People should be able to change the way they look.

Points:
- How you look is a personal decision; you can ignore what others think.

- People have always changed the way they look; wings are no different.

- Extreme changes are safe if they are done by doctors.

- _____

- _____

- _____

Against: People should not be able to change the way they look.

Points:
- Society must protect people from themselves, especially foolish young people.

- Although people like to change their appearance, they don't need to do it in permanent ways.

- Surgeons are not licensed to perform weird operations.

- _____

- _____

- _____

Debate strategy

When you debate, keep the attention of the audience by using unusual arguments. For example: pretend to agree with almost everything your opponent says, but then explain how this means they are wrong.

Say:
- "Well, of course, I agree that ... and ... and ... but that only means that my argument is correct because ... ."
- "Everything my opponent says sounds wonderful, except for the fact that ... ."

More ideas to debate

- Do you know people who have changed their bodies in some ways?
- What do you think about plastic surgery?
- Are there limits to what people should be able to do?
- Is age important in deciding about plastic surgery?

Learn more

Visit a health clinic, doctor's office or health website and find some information on plastic surgery, tattooing or other procedures. Read the materials and consider how ideas of safety, health and danger are shown in the text and pictures. Report what you find to your class.

Look online

Check out the website at www.read-and-think.com for extra learning resources.

Add new words to your personal dictionary on page 146.

Skills check

After finishing Unit 1, can you ...
- [ ] use dictionary skills to find the words you need to know?
- [ ] talk about Atlantis and mythology using examples and arguments?
- [ ] remember and use new exam skills and reading strategies?

After finishing Unit 2, can you ...
- [ ] use thesaurus skills to find synonyms and antonyms?
- [ ] talk about the Olympics in contemporary and historical times, discussing the pros and cons of international sporting events?
- [ ] remember and use new exam skills and reading strategies?

After finishing Unit 3, can you ...
- [ ] read letters efficiently and effectively, understanding the purpose of each part?
- [ ] talk about ideas related to evolution?
- [ ] understand different points of view about the exploration of space?
- [ ] remember and use new exam skills and reading strategies?

After finishing Unit 4, can you ...
- [ ] recognize and understand metaphors?
- [ ] talk about the creator of *The Lord of the Rings* and what the story stands for?
- [ ] remember and use new exam skills and reading strategies?

After finishing Unit 5, can you ...
- [ ] understand the role of commas and periods?
- [ ] talk about economics and evaluate the anti-globalization movement?
- [ ] remember and use new exam skills and reading strategies?

After finishing Unit 6, can you ...
- [ ] survey a passage to find the information you need?
- [ ] talk about the importance of money compared to other aspects of one's life?
- [ ] remember and use new exam skills and reading strategies?

After finishing Unit 7, can you ...
- [ ] recognize adjectives and adverbs and understand how they modify words in a sentence?
- [ ] talk about different theories about the extinction of the dinosaurs and relate them to threats to human life?
- [ ] remember and use new exam skills and reading strategies?

After finishing Unit 8, can you ...
- [ ] recognize and use phrasal verbs?
- [ ] talk about examples of famous lost treasures and how they were found?
- [ ] remember and use new exam skills and reading strategies?

After finishing Unit 9, can you ...
- [ ] recognize and use conjunctions correctly?
- [ ] talk about perspectives on history, specifically the Battle of Agincourt made famous in a Shakespeare play?
- [ ] remember and use new exam skills and reading strategies?

After finishing Unit 10, can you ...
- [ ] recognize and use contractions correctly?
- [ ] talk about the history and future of education at the university level?
- [ ] remember and use new exam skills and reading strategies?

After finishing Unit 11, can you ...
- [ ] recognize and use prepositions correctly?
- [ ] talk about extinction theories and their basis in fact?
- [ ] remember and use new exam skills and reading strategies?

After finishing Unit 12, can you ...
- [ ] recognize the correct use of colons, em-dashes and semi-colons?
- [ ] talk about the advantages and disadvantages of different techniques used to change people's appearances?
- [ ] remember and use new exam skills and reading strategies?

Exam strategies

1 When your read a multiple choice question, think of the answer before you look at the choices. Then choose the answer closest to what you thought.

2 When you study for an exam, make a list of all the things you find hard to remember. As you master each one, cross it off your list.

3 When you answer true and false questions, don't just look for the key words; read every word carefully. Sometimes an answer changes the meaning with a negative word, such as *not*.

4 In questions where you need to read a long passage, read the questions first so you know what you are looking for.

5 Multiple choice questions are often written with two or more answers that are almost identical. Look for the differences.

6 Before an exam, ask if you are allowed to make notes on the exam paper. If so, circle the key words in the questions and readings to help you remember.

7 Always come prepared to an exam with extra pencils, pens and erasers. Don't spend a long time carefully using correction fluid. Most teachers only care about your answers, so just cross out your mistakes and move on.

8 If you finish your exam early, use the time to go back and check your answers.

9 Always make sure you read the instructions carefully. Often, students overlook instructions such as *answer one of the three questions* and *answer all three*.

10 In essay questions, make sure your writing is easy to read. Don't rush so much that your letters turn into something that the teacher can't understand.

11 When preparing for an exam, it helps to study in the same atmosphere as the place you'll take the test. Study with good light at a desk or table with the music and TV turned off.

12 Measure the time you spend on each question according to the marks. If a question is worth 50%, spend 50% of your time on it. If it's only worth 10%, spend much less time.

Check your speed

Most of the readings in this book are around 300 words. Check how many words a minute you are reading and keep a record over the twenty-four main readings.

Minutes	1	2	3	4	5	6	7	8	9	10	11	12	13	14	15
300 words	300	150	100	75	60	50	43	38	33	30	27	25	23	21	20

Unit	1		2		3		4		5		6		7		8		9		10		11		12	
Lesson	1	2	1	2	1	2	1	2	1	2	1	2	1	2	1	2	1	2	1	2	1	2	1	2
Speed																								

Debate strategies

1. When you debate, make it very clear to yourself, your debate opponent(s) and everyone else who is listening, exactly what the debate is about—the *thesis*.

    Say:
    - "Today, I am (or *we are*) going to explain why ... ."

    Or begin with more of an introduction, explaining why it is important to debate the topic.
    - "Many of you will have read in newspapers the shocking story of ... .
    - Today I am (or *we are*) going to explain what should be done ... ."

    Repeat your thesis at the end of your argument, summarizing your points.

2. When you debate, try to give the point of view or some background to your argument, especially when it is based on a principle, system or theory of some kind.

    Say:
    - "Based on the principle that all people are equal ... ."
    - "As clearly shown in any democracy ... ."

3. When you debate, try to trap your opponents by thinking in advance about their arguments. Before they have a chance to explain their points, briefly say them and explain what is wrong with each one.

    Say:
    - "My opponent will probably try to tell you that ... but, it's obvious that ... ."
    - "I hope you are not going to try to suggest that ... . It's a foolish argument because ... ."

4. When you debate, use visual aids if they can help you make your point. Handouts, overhead transparencies or writing on a board are fine but make sure people are listening to you, not reading something else. Make your point quickly and clearly, explaining what you are talking about.

    Say:
    - "I just want to draw your attention to an important point here ... ."
    - "As the upper right-hand corner of the graph clearly shows ... ."

5. When you finish a debate, add a conclusion in which you explain how you have proved or disproved the thesis, depending which side you are on.

    Say:
    - "Finally, it is clear, based on the facts I have presented (list them), that ... ."
    - "Although my opponent has tried to make you think that ... my arguments (list them) have clearly proved that ... ."

6. When you debate, avoid telling long stories to support your ideas. Instead, try to use short summaries that make your point quickly. Rely on the audience's background knowledge. If you think most will know a story, you can just give the general outline and the reason you are telling it.

    Don't say:
    - "Once upon a time, there was a tortoise and a hare. They decided to have a race. The hare ... ."

    Say:
    - "Everyone knows the story of the race of the tortoise and the hare. It's the same story here where someone who thinks he is very skilled does not use those skills intelligently and ... ."

7 When you debate, use notes but don't write out every word of your presentation beforehand. Even if you memorize your speech, you will sound artificial. Make it easy on yourself by writing down numbered points and referring to them, for example, 1. climate change, 2. shelters, 3. meteorites.

Say:
- "I would like to make three points. My first point is that we would be able to predict massive climate change. My second point is that we would be able to prepare for it by building shelters. My third point is … ."

8 When you debate, always try to speak loudly and clearly. When you are debating in front of an audience, instead of talking to your opponent, talk to the audience. In a formal debate, they are the ones who will decide who has the better argument.

Say:
- "Let me explain to all of you … ."
- "I'd like each of you to understand that … ."
- "I know you will all agree with me that … ."

9 When you debate, always try to speak as if you are confident and know what you are talking about. Don't sound like you doubt what you are saying or may have thought something else before. Don't use expressions such as, *I think* or *I feel*.

Say:
- "This is the truth. The … ."
- "It has always been the case that … ."
- "There is absolutely no question that … ."

10 When you debate, don't bring your personal views and experiences into the argument. It's better to stick to the key points of your arguments.

Don't say:
- "Once when I was twelve years old, I had a similar problem … ."

Say:
- "Something that has happened to every twelve-year-old is … ."

11 When you debate, never say that you agree with your opponent or suggest there's a compromise between your two points. Make sure you are clearly supporting your points and attacking your opponent's throughout the debate.

Don't say:
- "I guess I never thought about that."
- "I suppose you have a good point there."
- "Maybe if we took part of what I say and part of what you say, we could … ."

Say:
- "This is no time for half-measures or compromises. We must all agree with my point that … ."

12 When you debate, keep the attention of the audience by using unusual arguments. For example: pretend to agree with almost everything your opponent says, but then explain how this means they are wrong.

Say:
- "Well, of course, I agree that … and … and … but that only means that my argument is correct because … ."
- "Everything my opponent says sounds wonderful, except for the fact that … ."

Personal dictionary

Use this page to keep a list of new words you discover in your reading. Write down the definitions if you need to, and then try to use each word in your writing and daily conversations in English.

Personal reading diary

Use this page to keep a list of what you read. As you read, try to answer these questions: What is the title? What is the genre (type of article, play or story)? What new vocabulary did I find? What strategies did I use to read it effectively? What did I learn from this? Did reading it change my mind in any way?

Title	Genre	Vocabulary	Strategies	I learned ...

Word list, by unit

Unit 1
bronze
ceramics
civilization
culturally
debate
devastating
discern
enslave
excavate
illustrate
iron
model
mythical
philosopher
poison
relate to
satisfaction
social
structures
supposedly
tidal wave

Unit 2
ancient
boxing
chariot
compete
creed
discus
disorganized
fence
funeral
high heels
honor
medal
modern
opponent
prohibited
sailing
score
sentence
strip
struggle
suit
trick
triumph
wrestling

Unit 3
bother
contemporary
buffet
curious
current
dilemma
essential
exchange
exhibition
exploration
frontier
ignorant
launch
massive
noble
outlandish
pioneer
reservation
shelter
telescope
venture

Unit 4
captivate
diverse
entrust
fantasy
hazardous
lodger
narrow-minded
recount
represent

Unit 5
activist
aspect
Buddhist
capitalism
dramatic
excessively
ironic
irrational
pilfer
private enterprise
production
simplicity
sole
standard of living
Third World
toil
totality
underdog
well-being
well-intentioned

Unit 6
affluent
countless
esteem
healthy
income
measure
moral
poverty
prosperous
pursue
safety
secret
source
study
virtuous
wealthy
wise

Unit 7
alternatively
bizarre
carnivore
comprehend
dragon
eruption
extinct
fossil
herbivore
imagine
incalculable
lava
lice
mammal
meteorite
parasite
perennial
record
reptile
scholar
specifically

Unit 8
accidentally
cask
ceramics
chamber
charcoal
delay
drill
hollow
item
manuscript
metal detector
mystery
parchment
pit
rare
reef
settlement
signal
solve
terracotta
vault

Unit 9
adapt
armor
arrow
band
bare
captor
combat
drown
exhausted
feat
jewelry
mobile
prisoner
rally
ransom
rouse
scavenge
seize
shall
vile
wound

Unit 10
admit
bachelor's degrees
ban
century
classical
college
controversy
curriculum
degree
doctorate
enroll
ideal
influence
institution
ivy
master's degree
rites
roots
studies
swiftly
turn out

Unit 11
abused
accumulate
age
cancer
cemented
circumstances
contaminate
decay
deduce
development
ecology
empire
estimates
expansion
extinction
food chain
gestation
habitat
influential
irrational
invasion
migration
mixture
monarchy
observation
pessimistic
pesticide
portion
propose
prosperity
resources
renown
revolution
scarce
source
species
theory
true
universal
valor

Unit 12
belly button
cautiously
combine
complication
desperate
diverse
extensive
evaluate
facility
horn
modify
outcast
plastic surgery
psychiatrist
qualifications
rib
waist
wrinkle

Word list, alphabetical

A
abused
accumulate
activist
adapt
admit
affluent
age
alternatively
ancient
armor
arrow
aspect

B
bachelor's degrees
ban
band
bare
belly button
bizarre
boxing
bronze
bother
Buddhist
buffet

C
cancer
capitalism
captivate
carnivore
cautiously
cemented
century
ceramics
chariot
circumstances
civilization
classical
college
combat
combine
compete
complication
comprehend
contaminate
contemporary
controversy
countless
creed
culturally
curious
current
curriculum

D
debate
decay
deduce
degree
delay
desperate
devastating
development
dilemma
discern
discus
disorganized
diverse
doctorate
dragon
dramatic
drill
drown

E
ecology
empire
enroll
enslave
entrust
eruption
essential
esteem
estimates
evaluate
excavate
excessively
exchange
exhausted
exhibition
expansion
exploration
extensive
extinct
extinction

F
facility
fantasy
feat
fence
food chain
fossil
frontier
funeral

G
gestation

H
habitat
hazardous
healthy
herbivore
high heels
honor
horn

I
ideal
ignorant
illustrate
imagine
incalculable
income
influence
influential
institution
invasion
iron
ironic
irrational
ivy

J
jewelry

L
launch
lava
lice
lodger

M
mammal
massive
master's degree
measure
medal
meteorite
migration
mixture
mobile
model
modern
modify
monarchy
moral
mythical

N
narrow-minded
noble

O
observation
opponent
outcast
outlandish

P
parasite
perennial
pessimistic
pesticide
philosopher
pilfer
pioneer
plastic surgery
poison
portion
poverty
prisoner
private enterprise
production
prohibited
propose
prosperity
prosperous
psychiatrist
pursue

Q
qualifications

R
rally
ransom
record
recount
relate to
renown
represent
reptile
reservation
resources
revolution
rib
rites
roots
rouse

S
safety
sailing
satisfaction
scarce
scavenge
scholar
score
secret
seize
sentence
shall
shelter
simplicity
social
sole
source
species
specifically
standard of living
strip
structures
struggle
study
studies
swiftly
suit
supposedly

T
telescope
theory
Third World
tidal wave
toil
totality
trick
triumph
true
turn out

U
underdog
universal

V
valor
vault
venture
vile
virtuous

W
waist
wealthy
well-being
well-intentioned
wise
wound
wrestling
wrinkle

149